THE WRITE STRUCTURE

THE WRITE STRUCTURE

THE TIMELESS STORYTELLING PRINCIPLES GREAT WRITERS USE TO CRAFT STORIES READERS LOVE

JOE BUNTING

THE WRITE PRACTICE

Copyright © 2021 by The Write Practice

All rights reserved.

No part of this book may be reproduced in any form or by any electronic or mechanical means, including information storage and retrieval systems, without written permission from the author, except for the use of brief quotations in a book review.

———

Get access to a host of downloadable tools and worksheets when you sign up at thewritepractice.com/structure.

For all the members of The Write Practice community. May you enjoy your writing, may it bring your life deep meaning, but most of all, may you finish your books.

CONTENTS

Introduction	1

PART I
WHY STRUCTURE

1. What If You Don't Like Structure?	11
2. Start Here: Dilemma	14
3. A Brief History of Story Structure	23

PART II
FUNDAMENTALS OF PLOT

4. Values	31
5. Subplots	42
6. Story Arcs: The 6 Shapes of Stories	50

PART III
ELEMENTS OF PLOT

7. Element 1: Exposition	75
8. Element 2: Inciting Incident	85
9. Element 3: Rising Action or Progressive Complications	97
10. Element 4: Dilemma	106
11. Element 5: Climax	113
12. Element 6: Denouement	129

PART IV
MAKING STRUCTURE WORK FOR YOUR WRITING

13. What to Do BEFORE You Start Structuring	141
14. Make Your Novel Idea Better	146
15. Find Your Plot Type	157
16. Plot Your Story In 18 Sentences	170
17. How to Write a Good First Chapter	181

Conclusion: Building a Definition of Stories	189
More Resources	191
Appendix A: Why Freytag's Technique Doesn't Work	193
Appendix B: Why You Shouldn't Use Falling Action in Your Story	205
Notes	209

INTRODUCTION

I'd like to tell you a secret. Something I've never told anyone, something no one but my wife knows.

Something that is mortifying.

Ready? Here goes.

I am a crier.

If there are two types of people in this world, people who cry in movies and people who don't, I'm the first type.

I cry over *every* movie.

Forrest Gump. Yep.

The Matrix. Cried over it.

Kung Fu Panda. Not once, not twice, but three times.

I can't help it.

And it's not just films. I cry when reading books. I once bawled while reading *The Boys in the Boat* in an airport, which is not a great place to have a breakdown since I kept expecting people to come up to me asking if I was safe.

I cry over television shows. Hodor's final scene in *Game of Thrones*? I was a wreck.

I've cried over commercials and YouTube videos.

I cry over HGTV shows. *Fixer Upper*? Don't even start.

Movie trailers are actually the worst, like little emotion bombs. After twenty minutes of them at a theater, I feel wrung out.

I don't want to cry. I'm not *trying* to cry. It would certainly be more convenient *not* to cry. It just happens.

There are a few exceptions, though, things that will keep my tear ducts from activating. I can't cry in stories that are boring, too dark or cynical, or too happy or light. But honestly every once in a while, even in the lamest juvenile story I've been forced to watch with my kids, I've felt my tear ducts start to burn.

Which is why it was so troubling when I read the first draft of my memoir, *Crowdsourcing Paris*, and realized that my eyes had been dry the whole time.

My tears respond to the moments of a story that are most powerful, but in my own book they weren't working.

Which meant my book wasn't working.

I was devastated.

I had already been working on this book for two years. Even more, by this point in my writing career, I had already written several books, including a book that would become a *Wall Street Journal* best-seller. I had studied creative writing in college, was part of a vibrant community of writers, many of whom were best-sellers, and had been a professional writer for the better part of a decade. Worse, I had been teaching writing on my website, The Write Practice, for five years.

I was helping a community of millions of people become better writers, but I had no idea how to help myself.

So when my friend Tim Grahl invited me to a workshop in New York taught by Shawn Coyne, the creator of Story Grid, a story structure framework, I had two thoughts:

1. *I already know this stuff well enough. Do I really need more?* and

2. *I'm desperate. I'll try anything if it can help me figure out what was wrong with my book.*

I flew up to New York City and sat in a classroom with thirty other people, including Stephen Pressfield, one of my favorite writers and the author of *Gates of Fire* and *The War of Art*.

Sitting there reminded me of my college screenwriting class with John Wilder, a veteran Hollywood screenwriter, who, on my first day of class, wrote on the board in bold letters, "STRUCTURE STRUCTURE STRUCTURE." When I got back my final project, it was covered with red ink and exclamation points.

I had already been learning about structure for years, from Wilder but also Blake Snyder's *Save the Cat* and Joseph Campbell's *The Hero with a Thousand Faces*, not to mention hundreds of novels, short stories, and films that I had studied and even broken down to their elements.

But it wasn't until that workshop that I finally realized what was wrong with my book.

It didn't have an emotion problem or a writing problem.

It had a structure problem.

And all the polishing and revision in the world wouldn't save it until I fixed the structure first.

That experience began a long exploration of plot. Not only did I revisit what I'd already learned about story structure, I discovered new sources too.

I learned from Robert McKee, the famed story workshop teacher and author of *Story*, who taught me about values and dramatic reversals.

I read *Freytag's Technique for the Drama*, the source of Freytag's Pyramid, one of the first plot diagrams, at least in the West.

I read Aristotle's *Poetics*, often cited as foundational to story structure theory but which I honestly found kind of vague and uninspiring.

I learned Randy Ingermanson's Snowflake Method, Dan

Harmon's Story Circle, Dan Wells' 7-Point Story Structure method, and a half-dozen other frameworks.

I read books, took online courses, went to live workshops.

So much of what I learned was helpful for my book and my storytelling in general.

But there were also a couple of problems that I ran into.

Sometimes, these frameworks contradicted each other. Or else used different language to describe the same thing.

Other times, their ideas made sense on paper, but when I went to apply them, they didn't work.

Other teachers had great ideas but weren't great teachers and I had to do extra work to fully understand them.

Many had theories that worked well for some kinds of stories, say sci-fi/fantasy stories, but not others, like contemporary romance or travel memoir.

Some story structure frameworks were for editors, not writers. Most writers don't need to know all the jargon and intricacies of a particular framework. It just weighs you down and distracts from the writing. Usually, you need just enough to write the next draft.

The biggest takeaway, though, was that not all stories are the same, which sounds obvious, but also all stories are made of the same things.

In this book, I want to share the things stories are made up of. I'll show you how you can arrange and dismantle and rearrange them in a way that works for the story you're trying to tell. And I'll try to bring together all the diffuse theory and grand ideas of all of the story gurus I've learned from into one simple process that you can put to practice in your writing immediately.

Why Are You Reading This?

That's what this book is about. Maybe, like me, you've learned a lot of theory about how stories work, and it still isn't working for you. Or maybe this is your first time learning about story structure.

The purpose of this book is not to spend hours learning storytelling jargon or to expound one more story structure framework that the world doesn't really need.

The purpose of this book is to get you writing. I want you to have your story idea ready to go by the end of this book. My goal is that when you finish reading this book—or maybe even after reading the first chapter—you'll have the tools you need to finish writing your next novel, memoir, screenplay, or short story.

Maybe you're reading this because you've written a book that's not working. Or maybe you're stuck in the middle of a book and need some ideas to help you keep writing. Maybe you've never written a book and aren't sure where to start.

Structure is the foundation of storytelling, and no matter where you are in the writing process, whether you're a seasoned writer or a complete novice, thinking about structure will help you solve the problems you're facing in your writing.

In this book, I want to go beyond theory. I want to give you something that works in practice. So that if you put it to use, it will actually help you write a better book, not at some point in the future, but *today*. I hope this will be the catalyst you need to take the next step, or maybe the first step, in your writing career.

Even better, I'll help you visualize these ideas in simple diagrams illustrated by a friend of mine, the talented artist and author Ross Boone. Because not everyone learns best through words. Sometimes a simple image can help you unlock a new concept that changes your writing forever.

My Gift to You

As I've said, this "Write Structure" process came out of my own experience trying to fix my own book.

After spending years relearning story structure, I applied it all to my own writing.

It was grueling, pound-your-head-on-your-desk work. It took two more years.

But the week before I was about to publish my book, I read it one last time. I was pacing in my living room late into the night, bent over my half-read manuscript, when it happened.

I wasn't trying. I wasn't forcing it. As always, it just happened of its own accord.

I cried.

There's nothing better than reading your book and realizing that *finally*, after everything you've put into it, all the problems you've fought over and pages you've wrestled with, it finally works.

That's the gift I want to give to you.

By the end of this book, I want you to be able to look at your book and see exactly what's not working.

But even more, I want you to be able to see the path to bringing it all together, so that you can feel that immense satisfaction too.

How to Use this Book

Story structure theory has been around for thousands of years, but even as the words and terms we use to talk about story structure have changed over the last few thousand years, the structure of actual, great stories has stayed remarkably consistent.

The intention of this resource is to sort through the ideas and principles from ancient philosophers to the latest Hollywood gurus to high-tower New York editors and present a universal framework that works for all stories. As a fellow writer, my goal is to help you find the structural tools that can transform your stories and then show you how to immediately apply them to your writing.

This book is divided into four parts.

Part one is about why plot structure matters, sharing the origins of story structure theory and what I think is the most helpful single aspect of plot structure and how to use it immediately.

Part two begins our exploration of the fundamentals of plot, which begins with the six universal values that make up the core of every story ever composed. Here we will also discuss two aspects that arise out this, including how subplots work and how the story's changing value shifts follow traditional patterns called story arcs.

Part three explores the final foundational aspect of story structure, the six elements of plot that you'll find in every story. You'll also get tips for how to find and enhance these elements in your own stories.

Part four gives a practical, step-by-step guide to using The Write Structure to create, outline, write, and revise your own story. This is geared mostly to novel writers, but all storytellers will be able to apply this to their own writing process.

At the end of each chapter you'll see a summary of key ideas as well as, in most chapters, a practice section where you can put the ideas you learned in that chapter to use immediately in your writing. I encourage you to not skip over these practice sections as they will help you internalize these ideas more quickly.

This book could not have been written without the story theorists and teachers who came before me. If there's anything in this book that helps you, assume it came from someone else. If there's anything in this book that's wrong, assume it came from me.

Finally, this is the second of what I hope will be many versions of this resource. Story structure is a rapidly advancing field, with new theories emerging every few years, and as they change how we think about structure, so too will this resource advance with them.

If you'd like updates when I release a new version of the book, and would like to get access to a host of downloadable tools and worksheets, you can sign up at thewritepractice.com/structure. There, I will be sending periodic updates about tools, content, and programs that you might find helpful in your own writing.

PART I

WHY STRUCTURE

Why does story structure matter? Will it really help you write your book? Is structure arbitrary or universal? And finally how can you put it to use now in your own writing?

In the first part of this book we are exploring this question of whether story structure, and particularly The Write Structure process, will really help you with your book. We'll look at the history of story structure theory and how it emerged from Aristotle to Freytag to modern theorists. We'll look at how different writers approach structure so you can find your own way to use the tools found in this book. And we'll also cover the single most important structural tool for your story, the dilemma.

1

WHAT IF YOU DON'T LIKE STRUCTURE?

You might be feeling some resistance to this idea that all you have to do to write a best-selling book is follow a rigid set of story structure principles.

You might even think writers who *do* focus on structure are sellouts, panderers who care more about making money than practicing the sacred craft of writing.

And if that's you, I get it. Writers, and all creatives, have always experienced a tension between creativity and established form. After all, the great Russian playwright Checkhov wrote a whole play about it, *The Seagull*.

Different writers have different attitudes about story structure. People tend to find themselves sorted into two groups, pantsers and plotters, and how you feel about structure separates you out into each group.

Plotters are people who structure out their entire books from beginning to end. They often even have long character profiles written for each person in their stories. They create detailed outlines. They have huge stacks of note cards. They know what's going to happen in each scene.

And then there are **pantsers**. Pantsers write by the seat of their pants. Pantsers don't *want* to know what's going to happen in their story. They might even feel like it's morally *wrong* to know what's going to happen, because it's going to ruin the magic.

Which type of writer are you?

But I think the pantser vs. plotter dilemma is *really* about something else entirely. I think the underlying issue is whether we should write from our head or by gut feeling.

Write with your head
vs.
Write with your gut

The plotters would say write with your head. The sum total of your knowledge, strategy, and planning work you do *before* you start writing creates the surest, most logical path to success with your story.

The pantsers would say write by gut feeling. The best ideas come from your intuition.

And what I would say is that both of them are only half-right.

I believe you need to write with your heart.

~~Write with your head~~
~~Write with your gut~~
Write with your heart

It's not enough to just write with your head. That will only lead to perfectionism, writer's block, and half-finished manuscripts that you quit writing because they don't live up to what you imagined. The stories produced by head-only writing are stilted, technically correct but lacking uniqueness, creativity, and life.

It's not enough to write with your gut either, which can lead to aimless writing that veers into tangents without ever developing anything.

In order to write a book readers will love, you need to put *all of yourself* into your writing. Head, gut, and **heart**. What that means is you need to learn some simple principles, principles that have proven to lead to successful stories over thousands of years.

But you also need to write with your gut, because it's your gut that gives you the drive to actually finish things. It's your gut that delivers unexpected ideas, the kind where you don't really know where they came from; they just *work*.

ALL of this, though, needs to be centered in your heart, where the two of those converge.

Your head needs to descend into your heart. Your gut feelings need to rise into your heart.

Your heart needs to lead your writing process.

It is *this* that makes great writers, painters, sculptors, musicians, songwriters, and other artists. They have the training, but they also engage their gut feelings, and they center it all in their hearts.

And that's what the Write Structure process is about: engaging your whole self, your mind, your gut, but most of all, your heart.

Your writing deserves nothing less than *all* of you.

Key Ideas

- There are two types of writers: pantsers, people who write by gut feeling (by the seat of their pants, in other words); and plotters, people who write with their heads and like to have everything plotted out before they start writing.
- The best way to write is not from your head or your gut but from your heart.
- Both pantsers and plotters will benefit from the Write Structure process when they write with their hearts.

2

START HERE: DILEMMA

Plot structure can be overwhelming, and this is especially problematic for the writer who wants to *finish* something, not learn esoteric principles and complex terminology.

The goal of the Write Structure process is to make this as simple as possible, so you can move from *learning* to *writing* immediately.

With that in mind, it matters where you begin. Because if you only take one idea away from this process, this is the one that will most transform your writing.

So where should we begin? As I've explored the world of story structure, there's one concept that has most changed my perspective on storytelling and brought life to my writing.

Dilemma.

What is a dilemma? And how does it work in your story?

Dilemma Definition

A dilemma is the moment in a story when a character is faced with a difficult choice between two either good or bad things.

How Dilemma Works in Your Story

We begin with dilemmas because dilemmas center stories.

Great stories are built around a single, overarching choice. The entire story builds to this dilemma. And the denouement, the story's resolution, falls away from this dilemma. The climax, the highest point of action in the story, emerges directly from the dilemma. Which is all to say: if you don't have a dilemma, you don't have a story.

We will cover dilemmas in depth in Chapter 6, including *why* dilemmas are the central element of your story (so if you don't want to take my word for it, you can skip ahead), but here, I want to give you a simple crash course in dilemmas so you can start seeing them in the stories you love most and using them in your writing.

Story Dilemma Case Studies

At the same time, as I've taught these concepts over the years, I've found that dilemmas tend to confuse people. The idea of a *choice* being the central storytelling element seems to be baffling.

The fastest way to see how dilemmas actually work is to learn from examples from popular stories.

Romeo and Juliet

Let's begin with William Shakespeare's *Romeo and Juliet*, the quintessential romantic tragedy, by taking a look at how dilemma works in this story, starting with a brief synopsis.

Synopsis

Romeo and Juliet is the tale of two lovers from feuding families. The couple elopes in secret, but when Romeo kills Juliet's cousin in revenge for killing his best friend, Romeo is forced into exile. Not knowing that Juliet is now married, her family makes plans for her to marry. To escape the betrothal, Juliet takes an elixir that puts her in a deep sleep, mimicking death, and sends a note to Romeo promising to find him when she awakes. The message goes astray, and Romeo races to Verona to see his dead wife. When he arrives at her tomb, Romeo gives her a last kiss before taking poison to end his life. Juliet wakes up to find Romeo dying, and takes his dagger and stabs herself in the heart, dying. Their two families find their deceased children and decide to end their feud.

What is the Dilemma?

So what is the dilemma in *Romeo and Juliet*? Look at the summary above and see if you can spot the choice the couple makes.

When I ask students this, they usually respond with something like love vs. family or duty vs. love.

However, as it relates to story structure, the dilemma is much more specific. There is just one core moment where the young couple is faced with a dilemma that turns the whole story.

Have you found it yet? I'll give you a hint:

When he arrives at her tomb, Romeo gives her a last kiss before **deciding** to take poison to end his life. Juliet wakes up to find Romeo dying, and **decides** to take his dagger and stabs herself in the heart, dying.

That's right. The dilemma Romeo and Juliet are faced with occurs just before the climactic moment when both Romeo and Juliet commit suicide.

You might phrase it like this:

Dilemma: to live in a world without the other *OR* to join each other in the afterlife by ending their lives.

Considering the events of the story and the characters themselves, that's a tough decision, right?

Should Romeo simply continue his life knowing that his love is dead? Should he go back to normal after the thing that gave him purpose is gone? You might say, *Yes, of course!* But faced with that situation, you too might consider making another choice, if only for a moment.

And for Juliet, seeing her husband dead in her arms, his dagger just next to him, knowing that her own failed plan was the thing that led him to his death, it is perfectly conceivable that she would choose to follow her husband into the afterlife. Of course, she could also instead decide to go to her parents and in-laws and show them what they've done through their feud, dedicating the rest of her life to her husband's memory. We, the audience, watching this unfold, certainly see the potential in her life and *want* her to go on living. At the same time, we see the difficulty in a life like that, the hardship and loneliness of it. Maybe being with her lover in eternity really would be the best way to go.

And *that*, exactly right there, is the power of dilemma. The choice hanging in the air, the moment of decision. Which way will the character go? This way or that? You can imagine Shakespeare's audience shouting at the stage when it was first performed, "Don't do it. Stop, she's just sleeping!" The *drama* of it all, powered by nothing more than two choices.

One important thing to point out here is *where* the dilemma fits into the story.

Take a look at the plot diagram of *Romeo and Juliet* below.

Don't worry if you don't fully understand everything in this diagram. We're going to build up our understanding of plot diagrams over the course of this book, but what I want you to see is *where* the dilemma occurs.

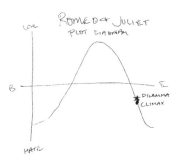

A story's dilemma happens before the climax, usually toward the end of the story. While there are certainly stories that have the climax in the second act, just to the right of the center of the story, for *most* stories, the climax occurs in the final act, and usually within the last three scenes.

Frozen

Now that we've seen the dilemma at work in *Romeo & Juliet*, let's look at another example, this time from one of the most popular animated films of all time.

Synopsis *Spoilers*

The Disney film *Frozen* is the story of two sisters, Princess Elsa and Princess Anna of Arendelle, who are orphaned at a young age. When Anna and Elsa get into a fight that results in Elsa unleashing an eternal winter with her magical power to control and create ice and snow, it leads to Anna getting struck in the crossfire, causing her heart to "freeze." To avoid being turned to ice, Anna must experience an act of true love, but when she's betrayed by her fiancé, Hans, who then seeks to kill Elsa and end the eternal winter, she has to choose between saving herself or sacrificing herself to save her sister. She chooses to save her sister, turning to ice in the process. But Anna's sacrifice, counting as an act of true love, thaws her, and the sisters reunite.

What is the Dilemma?

Did you find the dilemma yet?

Remember, a dilemma is a difficult choice between two things.

In this case, the choice is as follows:

Should Anna save herself and allow her sister to be killed, or should she save her sister, sacrificing herself in the process?

What is so great about *Frozen* is that it sets up this dilemma with a perfect visual:

Anna stands in the snowstorm. To her left, Kristoff races toward her to save her with "true love's kiss." To her right, Hans is about to kill Elsa. She is stuck in the middle, nearly completely frozen, both by her affliction and by the choice she has to make.

Which should she choose?

Both are bad options.

She can choose only one.

And we, the audience, are completely wrapped up in the drama of the scene.

"Mysteries are powerful because they create a need for closure," says Robert Cialdini.

What the dilemma does is open a knowledge gap between what we *know* is going to happen and what we *don't* know.

This is the power of dilemma. It activates our curiosity. It is the force in a story that leaves us on the edge of our seats, desperate to find out what's going to happen next.

Where Dilemmas Happen in Your Story

Where do dilemmas happen in a story?

In the examples above, you can see how important it is to have a major dilemma, which usually takes place close to the end of a story, just before the crisis.

But there's a secret about the dilemma that can transform your story.

Because not only does your story need to have a dilemma, but to have drama, dilemmas need to be distributed *throughout* your story. In fact, the following is true:

Every scene must have a dilemma.

Every act must have a dilemma.

Every book must have a dilemma.

Which means dilemmas are not just a useful tool. Dilemmas are the foundation of your story.

We will talk more about dilemmas and where they occur in Chapter 6, but for our purposes now, one of the best ways that you can improve your story is to make sure you have dilemmas, that they occur frequently, and that they grow in consequence as the story goes on.

When we talk about how a dilemma must occur in every scene and act, you might be thinking, "Well what *is* a scene? What is an act? And how does that relate to chapters?"

If you're familiar with these terms, skip the next section, but for those who aren't sure what we're talking about, here's a brief explanation of scenes and acts.

Scene vs. Chapter vs. Act

What are scenes, chapters, and acts, and how are they different from each other?

A scene depicts a single story event. Scenes vary in length anywhere from 500 to 10,000 words, but tend to fall in the 1,500 to 2,500 word range. In screenwriting terminology, a scene takes place in a single setting and period of time, but in novel writing, a scene may cross several settings and may even contain short time jumps as long as it depicts a single story event. Good scenes convey the six structure elements found in Chapter 6.

A chapter is an arbitrary division of a book. Writers can choose to make their chapters as long or as short as they like. Chapters can include multiple scenes or even break a scene up into more than one chapter. Since it is an arbitrary choice, we do not use the term "chapter" to describe a story's structure.

Acts are a method of dividing stories into broad sections. The most common structural theory is the three-act story structure, which divides stories in the beginning, middle, and end—act one, act two, and act three. Not an arbitrary distinction, acts have specific rhythms and structural components that we will explore in Chapter 6. By length and/or number of scenes, act one tends to contain twenty-five percent of the story, act two fifty percent of the story, and act three twenty-five percent.

How do you write a dilemma, practically?

Dilemmas are questions, and since those questions are happening in a character's head, they usually occur "off page" or "off screen." In other words, while they will occasionally be written out explicitly, usually they're implied but not clearly posed on the page.

But even if the dilemma is happening off page, you the writer still need to know what the literary dilemma is in every story, and potentially, every scene you write.

When you're outlining your story or you're about to write a scene, start by figuring out what the dilemma will be.

Start by asking what choice the character will be faced with.

Remember to make it *difficult*. A choice between something good and something bad is no choice at all. For example, if you push your character to choose between getting $1,000 or eating a bowl of slugs, that's not a real choice.

Instead, make the choice between two *good* things or two *bad* things to make that choice into a true dilemma.

Then, write your scene or act or story so that it builds to that choice. I often find myself asking, what events will lead up to this choice? How can I put my character in a place where they're struggling with a dilemma like this?

Key Ideas

- Dilemma is the most useful element of plot for writers, and the central piece of the Write Structure process.

- A dilemma in a story is a moment in a story when a character is faced with a difficult choice between two either good or bad things.
- Every plot, act, and scene should have a dilemma.

Practice

Dilemma Exercise: Find a scene in one of your favorite books or films and evaluate it. Does it have a dilemma? What is that dilemma? Write it out, stating what the choice is in the following formula:

_____ must make the difficult choice between _____ (choice) and _____ (consequence of that choice, e.g. suffer, experience, etc) OR _____ and _____ (consequence of that choice, e.g. suffer, experience, etc).

3

A BRIEF HISTORY OF STORY STRUCTURE

Where did story structure come from? Is it something people thought up to make things more difficult for writers?

The first to theorize that well-composed stories had any kind of structure, at least in the West, was Aristotle, the Greek philosopher from the third century BC. In an essay called *Poetics*, he argued that good stories had a beginning, a middle, and an end, and he talked a bit about what should be in each part.

If that sounds kind of obvious, you're right. Much has been said about the profundity of Aristotle's story structure advice, and perhaps saying anything about story structure in the third century BC is profound. Honestly, though, I wouldn't read *Poetics* for writing tips.

A few hundred years later, at around 16 AD, Horace, a Roman playwright, said all good plays should be five acts, no more, no less. His advice wasn't much more expansive than that, and there was very little direction as to the contents of those five acts. He spent as much ink arguing for state censorship, *deus ex machina* (now a mortal sin of storytelling), and a cast of no more than three characters. Which is to say, perhaps we should treat his plot structure advice with skepticism.

But perhaps it was from Horace that the editors who added the act labels to the plays of Shakespeare took their mandate. William Shakespeare did not, in fact, set his plays intentionally into five acts, or if he did, he did not label them that way. Instead, his first editor, Nicholas Rowe, thinking he was making Shakespeare more accessible, added these divisions, perhaps arbitrarily, at the same time providing the five-act structure with its archetype.

Still, it wasn't until the mid-1800s that plot diagrams truly began to take shape, when a German playwright and novelist named Gustav Freytag published everything he knew about story in one book called *Freytag's Technique of the Drama* and changed the way people thought about stories for the next 150 years.

He became a staunch advocate of the five-act structure, giving extensive descriptions for what should be in each act. Here, finally, is someone who could actually give some sound writing advice, some of which actually holds up more than 150 years later! He also published the first plot diagram. Here it is straight out of *Freytag's Technique*:

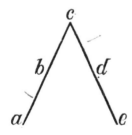

These parts of the drama, (*a*) introduction, (*b*) rise, (*c*) climax, (*d*) return or fall, (*e*) catastrophe, have each what is peculiar in purpose and in construction.

Looks a bit like a pyramid, right? You might almost call it ... Freytag's Pyramid.

Since then, this plot diagram has become the dominant

framework for understanding story structure. It is taught everywhere from middle schools to high schools to creative writing seminars throughout the world.

And as it has proliferated, it has transformed from the above triangle to the following hat shape:

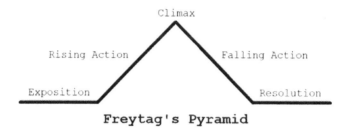

And, sometimes, to something more mountainous:

Please note that neither Gustav Freytag nor The Write Practice endorse any of these iterations. More on that later.

As the shape of the Freytag's Pyramid has changed, so too have the elements of Freytag's five-act structure, as the chart below shows. Note the subtle shift in language: from introduction which contains an exposition to exposition outright; from rising movement to rising action; from Freytag's catastrophe to the much more flexible, if vague, resolution.

Freytag's Five Act Structure
1. Introduction
   a. Exposition
   b. Inciting Incident
2. Rising Movement
3. Climax
4. Falling Action
   a. Force of the Final Suspense
5. Catastrophe

Five Modern Plot Points*
1. Exposition
   a. Inciting Incident
2. Rising Action
3. Climax
4. Falling Action
5. Resolution or Denouement

* These are the most frequently taught plot points, but many theories have synonymous terms or different structures entirely.

But despite more than 150 years of storytelling, including the invention of film, television, and other story forms, the foundational plot diagram has been taught in largely the same way since Freytag's first drawing.

However, with the advancement of film and the rise of Hollywood, plus better understanding of the ideas of Joseph Campbell and his monomyth, there has been a dramatic change in plot diagrams and story structure. This transformation has occurred over the last forty years, and while often not reflected in how story is taught in schools (but should be), it has been transformative in the writing community.

Chiefly begun by Robert McKee, advanced by Shawn Coyne of Story Grid, and innovated upon by Dan Harmon, K. M. Weiland, and others, plot diagrams and story structure have emerged into a golden age.

However, with great innovation can come great chaos. This has occurred within the story structure community, with story theorists providing different terms for the same principles, the same terms for *different* principles, contradictory information, and more. I've studied more than a dozen plot diagram frameworks and taught many to the members of my writing community, and I've seen firsthand how much confusion competing theories can cause.

That's why over the last several years, I've been establishing a simplified, unified theory primarily for creative writers called The Write Structure. It's a writing practice that brings together what actually works in all the major storytelling theories and principles and provides a standardized language that can be understood by all.

Here is Freytag's original Five-Act Structure compared with the Five Modern Plot Points that are largely taught today, especially in schools, and finally, The Write Structure.

We will talk more about The Write Structure's plot diagram later on in this guide, as it's very different from the original five-act structure taught by Freytag, while salvaging the integrity of what makes structure in a story so important.

Note too that the plot diagram is just one piece of our understanding of story structure, which begins with the foundational values at the core of all storytelling.

But before we explore that in the next chapter, let me end our discussion of the history of story structure by talking about where we see The Write Structure's role in it. Our purpose is not to replace other story structure frameworks, but to centralize them and make them accessible to the writer who is just trying to finish a great book.

Furthermore, as our understanding of story structure advances, so too will this framework, deepening in layers while maintaining its simplicity.

With that in mind, let's begin.

Key Ideas

- Aristotle was the first recorded story structure theorist, suggesting stories have a beginning, middle, and end.
- Gustave Freytag invented the first recorded plot

diagram, a pyramid shape, with the plot points exposition, inciting incident, rising movement, climax, and falling action.
- Others have evolved plot structure theory including Robert McKee, Shawn Coyne, K.M. Weiland, and more.
- The Write Structure exists to make story structure theory simple and practical for the working writer.

PART II

FUNDAMENTALS OF PLOT

Plot is a sequence of events in a story in which the main character is put into a challenging situation that forces them to make increasingly difficult choices. These choices drive the story toward a climactic event and resolution, and increase in tension and death stakes as the plot advances.

Plot and structure go hand-in-hand, but where the plot is unique to the writer's creation, the structure is a pattern that, in a reader's subconscious, sets up expectations for how a story's sequence of events will unfold—even if they don't realize it in the moment.

You can think of plot and structure like the DNA of your story. Without them, no story can exist.

4

VALUES

At the most basic level, stories are about values in conflict. If you've been writing creatively for any amount of time, you've probably heard you need conflict in your stories, that no matter what kind of story you're writing—a novel, short story, children's book, graphic novel, or script—you need conflict to keep the plot interesting and exciting.

But what does that really mean?

You might think creating conflict means you need to show spectacular events: a car chase, an argument between lovers, a fistfight, or the threat of a nuclear explosion. Or you might think of conflict as some kind of internal experience: suffering, depression, longing, or pain.

But the truth is that events and emotions aren't what produce great conflict that propels stories. If those are the only elements of conflict in your stories, you'll have some pretty flat stories.

Conflict, in good stories, is not about spectacular events or painful emotions.

Good conflict is about values.

Value Definition

Value, according to the Oxford English Dictionary, is the regard that something is held to deserve; the importance, worth, or usefulness of something.

In other words, a value is something you admire, something you want. If you value something, it means you *think it's good*.

Values in Stories

Here are some examples of things you might value:

- Money
- Friends
- A sibling
- Education
- Organization
- Justice
- Compassion
- Ferraris
- Environment
- Honor
- Courage
- Productivity
- Power
- Humility

This could easily become a never-ending list.

But if you think about it, every value can be distilled to six essential human values.

Building off of Maslow's Hierarchy of Needs, these values are as follows:

1. **Survival from Nature.** The value of life. Because if you don't have your life, you don't have much.
2. **Safety, or Survival from Others.** Surviving crime, other people, even monsters, you could say.
3. **Love/Community.** The value of human connection.
4. **Esteem.** The value of your status and hierarchy within a community.
5. **Self-actualization.** The value of reaching your potential.
6. **Transcendence.** The value of going beyond yourself to discover a larger purpose.

Credit to Robert McKee for first making this connection (as far as I'm aware) in his book *Story*, and to Shawn Coyne, the author of *Story Grid*, for introducing me to it.

You might be wondering, well, that's interesting, but what does it have to do with telling a great story? Hang with me for one second, and I'll show you.

Once you have these six values, you turn them into scales with the positive value on one side and its inverse on the opposite side.

Here are the six value scales, as they relate to the six core values:

1. Survival from Nature > Life vs. Death
2. Survival from Others > Life vs. a Fate Worse than Death
3. Love/Community > Love vs. Hate
4. Esteem > Accomplishment vs. Failure
5. Personal Growth > Maturity vs. Naïveté
6. Transcendence > Good vs. Evil

Here's an example of what a value scale can look like:

And this is where this connects with story, because these are the same values that drive good storytelling.

In fact, you can take these value scales and map them to different types of stories.

Plot Types

As stories evolved over thousands of years, they began to fall into patterns called plot types. These types tend to operate on the same underlying values. They also share similar structures, characters, and what Robert McKee calls obligatory scenes.

How should you determine plot type? Based on the value scale.

Here are the six value scales and how they relate to many of the most common types of stories:

1. **Life vs. Death:** Action, Adventure Stories
2. **Life vs. a Fate Worse than Death:** Thriller, Horror, Mystery Stories
3. **Love vs. Hate:** Romance, Love Stories
4. **Accomplishment vs. Failure:** Performance, Sports Stories

5. **Maturity vs. Naïveté:** Coming-of-Age Stories
6. **Good vs. Evil:** Temptation, Morality Stories

These plot types transcend genre. You can have a sci-fi love story, a historical thriller, or a fantasy performance story, a mystery romance story, or even a young adult adventure story.

Your story's plot type will determine much of your story: the scenes you must include, the conventions and tropes you employ, your characters (including protagonists, side characters, and antagonists), and more.

While most popular stories will fit within the thirteen plot types above, you could also get more specific by exploring subtypes. Subtypes are more specific plots with unique conventions, tropes, and characters. Examples of subtypes include revenge plots, a subtype of action plots; heist plots, a subplot of adventure stories; or obsession love stories. Most stories that work will fall somewhere into the above plot types, and *all* stories that work will fall into the six value scales.

However, the plot type itself is determined by the core value scale of your story.

Plot Type Examples

Before we continue, let's look at a couple of examples to see how value scales and plot types work practically, starting with *The Hobbit* by J.R.R. Tolkien, one of the best-selling novels of all time.

The Hobbit

When you're trying to understand the type of story you're trying to tell, the first question to ask is the following:

What value scale most determines the story's plot advancement? Or, in most of the story's scenes, what human value changes from the beginning of the scene to the end?

When I ask my writing students this question, they most

frequently mention life vs. death, good vs. evil, and sometimes maturity vs. naïveté.

Ultimately, most scenes in *The Hobbit* fall on the life vs. death scale.

This poses the repetitive question (driving the main plot of the story): "Is Bilbo Baggins going to survive the adventure with the dwarves?"

That means *The Hobbit*, at its core, is an adventure story, which means that the majority of the scenes move on the life vs. death scale.

At the same time, there are definitely moments of good vs. evil in *The Hobbit* as well, especially in the final climactic scene, when (spoiler, but it's almost one hundred years old, so that's on you) Thorin and the dwarves go treasure-mad, forcing Bilbo to make a choice about whose side he's going to be on.

But while the good vs. evil temptation is much more present in Tolkien's following series, *The Lord of the Rings*, it makes up just a few scenes in *The Hobbit*, which means it's not the main value scale.

Instead, the main value scale is life vs. death.

Twilight

Let's talk about another example, this time *Twilight* by Stephenie Meyer.

What is the main value scale of this best-selling paranormal young adult novel?

For *Twilight*, many people guess: life vs. a fate worse than death, love vs. hate, and maturity vs. naïveté.

There are varying levels of all of these values present in this novel, but the main value scale is this:

Love vs. hate.

It's a love story, in other words.

The question that permeates most of the scenes in Twilight is, "Will Bella and Edward get together in the end? Or will circumstance, outside forces, and their own issues keep them apart?"

Will love win by the end of this story, or will hate?
Catcher in the Rye
Let's look at one more example, *Catcher in the Rye*.
Looking at our value scales and plot types which best describes J.D. Salinger's classic young adult novel?

1. **Life vs. Death:** Action, Adventure Stories
2. **Life vs. a Fate Worse than Death:** Thriller, Horror, Mystery Stories
3. **Love vs. Hate:** Romance, Love Stories
4. **Accomplishment vs. Failure:** Performance, Sports Stories
5. **Maturity vs. Naïveté:** Coming-of-Age Stories
6. **Good vs. Evil:** Temptation, Morality Stories

This one is easier, right? It's a coming of age story.

The conflict at the heart of most of the scenes in *Catcher in the Rye* is between Holden Caulfield's growing sophistication as a young, cynical prep school drop out and his immaturity, his naïveté, because he is still in many ways a child.

As you attempt to better understand the stories you are trying to write, consider the values at their core. Knowing the value scale of your main plot can inform the choices you make throughout the writing process. We'll explore how later in this book.

Consider too your plot type, which can sometimes be more apparent, depending on the story you're trying to tell. By knowing the values at work behind your plot type, you will be better able to tap into them as you write.

Best-Selling Value Scales vs. Literary Value Scales

While you consider the plot types and value scales of the story you're trying to tell, consider how those values will work in the storytelling marketplace.

Best-selling books tend to come from these four value scales:

Best-Selling Value Scales

1. **Life vs. Death:** Action, Adventure Stories
2. **Life vs. a Fate Worse than Death:** Thriller, Horror, Mystery/Crime
3. **Love vs. Hate:** Romance, Love Stories
4. **Accomplishment vs. Failure:** Performance, Sports Stories

Think about it: crime novels, thrillers, fantasy and science fiction adventure stories, sports novels, romance novels. These are the cliché best-sellers, and for good reason. They're about deeply held, universal values that all of us hold as fundamental to our lives.

In our own lives, if you dip too low on any one of these value scales, at best, you'll end up in therapy; at worst, in the hospital (or the grave)!

Life, safety, belonging, accomplishment. These values are essential to our lives.

They are also the values of most best-selling books.

That doesn't mean that all good stories come from these values. Many great stories, some of which win major literary awards, come from the two remaining value scales:

1. **Maturity vs. Naïveté:** Coming-of-Age Stories
2. **Good vs. Evil:** Temptation, Morality Stories

These are what Shawn Coyne calls "internal" values.

External values, like life, safety, love, and accomplishment, all come from outside the individual. Internal values, though, like maturity and morality, all exist within the individual.

Some of the most revered stories in history, stories that are taught in schools and win top prizes, have internal values at their core.

But these stories do not tend to be best-sellers. Why? Perhaps because they're less universal and more specific to each person and culture. Perhaps because they are much more personal, dealing with the internal parts of a character's life rather than the external. Internal values tend to drive the main plots of memoirs and literary novels, not genre-based, mass market books. This isn't always true, and of course there are many notable exceptions.

However, as an author, you have to decide what kinds of stories you want to write. Do you want to write a best-selling book about major external values? Or do you want to write a story that's more internally driven?

Best-Selling Stories Are About Values In Conflict

Your story needs conflict, but good conflict doesn't mean more arguments and car chases.

The kind of conflict your stories need more of is between values, and the way to master any type of story is to put the story's main value in conflict with its opposite.

If you're writing an adventure story, that means you need to have life and death moments.

If you're writing a thriller, you need to have moments of life vs. a fate worse than death.

If you're writing a love story, you need to have as many moments of negative love, of anger, disillusion, and even hatred, as you do love.

If you're writing a sports story, there have to be as many moments of near failure, or actual failure, as there are of success.

If you're writing a coming-of-age story, then you need to

include moments where the growing maturity of the character is put into conflict with its opposite, naïveté.

And finally, if you're writing a temptation or morality story, you need moments of temptation, where the character genuinely considers whether to take actions they know are wrong because of how it might benefit them or solve a greater problem.

Bad Stories Have No Values or Too Many Values

Bad books? Stories that don't work don't know what their values are.

Or they're trying to have every single value possible.

You can't do that if you want to tell a great story. You have to choose! If you want to master the type of story you're trying to tell, start with finding the story's value.

In Chapter 10, we will talk more about how to use this scale to improve your story.

But can you have a story have more than one value scale? Continue to the next chapter to find out.

Key Ideas

- At their core, stories are about six core values: life, safety, love, success, self-actualization, and transcendence.
- These core values align with plot types, and the value at the center of each plot type must drive most of the scenes in a plot of that type.
- Stories go wrong when they aren't clear on their core value, when they choose too many values, or when they don't focus on values at all.
- There are external values (life, safety, love, and esteem) and internal values (self-actualization and

morality). Best-selling stories tend to focus on external values and literary stories tend to focus on internal values.

Practice

Values Exercise: Analyze three of your favorite novels or films. What is their plot type and value scale?

5

SUBPLOTS

Good stories always contain one core plot. The core plot contains the main conflict that drives the entire story. It informs your character choices, key scenes, tone, and more.

However, most novels, films, television serials, and other storytelling forms have multiple plotlines, almost always two and sometimes three, including:

- The external plot
- The internal plot
- The subplot

In the previous chapter we discussed internal and external plots. Now let's focus on subplots.

Stories are complicated, twisting, multifaceted things. At some point, in many of the *best* stories, it feels like everything is complete chaos, and then, seemingly all at once, it's as if the chaos has come to a head in a way that makes everything line up perfectly.

Great writers do this intentionally, weaving tension into their stories and then paying it off at the exact right moment.

To do this, one of the *best* tools in a writer's toolbox is the subplot.

But what is a subplot? How can you spot it in the books and stories you love most? And if you're a writer, how do you use it to tell better stories?

Subplot Definition

A subplot is a secondary storyline, or plot, within a story that supports the main plot. It may involve the main characters and/or may involve characters associated with them.

The Most Popular Types of Subplots

By far, the most present and popular subplots across all genres of stories are . . .

Any guesses?

Love stories.

Love plots fit perfectly into almost every kind of story, from thrillers to adventure stories and even love stories themselves (*Pride and Prejudice*, for example).

Their pervasiveness is so extreme that subplots are almost synonymous with love plots.

Examples of love story subplots span from classics to modern best-sellers, including:

- *The Hunger Games* by Suzanne Collins
- *Crime and Punishment* by Fyodor Dostoevsky
- *Pride and Prejudice* by Jane Austen
- *A Tale of Two Cities* by Charles Dickens
- *The Alchemist* by Paulo Coelho
- *The Lord of the Rings* by J.R.R. Tolkien
- *Anne of Green Gables* by Lucy Maud Montgomery
- *War and Peace* by Leo Tolstoy

- *Harry Potter and the Goblet of Fire* by J.K. Rowling (and every subsequent book in the series—it took her to book four to fit one in though!)
- *The Catcher in the Rye* by J.D. Salinger
- *The Perks of Being a Wallflower* by Stephen Chbosky
- *Gone Girl* by Gillian Flynn
- *Ready Player One* by Ernest Cline
- *Frozen* (Disney film)
- *Crazy Stupid Love* (film)

And many more.

The proliferation of love story subplots make sense, especially from a commercial perspective, since the romance genre is one of the most commercially successful genres. Having a romantic element in the story can spice up the plot and sales, as all of us understand what it's like to want to be intimately loved.

All that being said, authors are by no means required to use a love story subplot if they don't want to, and many of the most successful books of all time, both from a literary and commercial perspective, do *not* involve romance.

Other types of subplots include mystery, horror, adventure, performance, and even buddy plots, which are love stories centered on friendship instead of romantic love (for example, *Butch Cassidy and the Sundance Kid* or even *Toy Story*).

Subplots Center On Values

As we've talked about elsewhere, stories center around six core value scales:

1. Life vs. Death
2. Life vs. a Fate *Worse* than Death
3. Love vs. Hate

4. Accomplishment vs. Failure
5. Maturity vs. Naïveté
6. Good vs. Evil

The love story subplot sits on the love vs. hate value scale. An adventure story, on the other hand, would rest on the life vs. death scale, but might have a love story subplot, like Katniss and Peeta in *The Hunger Games*.

When analyzing stories, finding the core values of the subplot and core plot can help you discover what kind of subplot is supporting the story's main arc.

Why Subplots Are So Useful

How do you find a subplot though? And how can you tell the difference between the main plot and the subplot?

Stories tend to drag in the middle. Subplots were invented by enterprising writers to add intrigue to the story and keep it moving when things got slow.

And they work!

That's why you can often find subplots in the second act, after the inciting incident and the protagonist's acceptance of their call to action. Subplots pick up the pace just when tension starts to slow down, as you'll see in the next chapter.

Where Subplots Fit Within a Story

A traditional three-act story has one core element of each type, but it also has each element in every act, as so:

Act 1: Introduce the world and characters, and begin the main plot

- **Core Exposition**
- **Core Inciting Incident**

- Rising Action
- Dilemma
- Climax
- Denouement

Act 2: Complicate the plot through the rising action

- Exposition
- Inciting Incident
- **Core Rising Action**
- **Core Dilemma**
- Climax
- Denouement

Act 3: Pay off the plot with the climax and resolution

- Exposition
- Inciting Incident
- Rising Action
- Core dilemma
- **Core Climax**
- **Core Denouement**

I've marked the six elements of the **core** plot above. However, as you can see, there are more instances of exposition and rising action than there are core plots. These additional sections of exposition and rising action are, to some degree, filled by the subplot.

See below:

Act 1: Introduce the world, characters, and begin the main plot

- **Core Exposition**
- **Core Inciting Incident**
- Rising Action

- Dilemma
- Climax
- Denouement

Act 2: Complicate the plot through the rising action

- Subplot Exposition
- Subplot Inciting Incident
- **Core Rising Action** Subplot Rising Action
- **Core Dilemma**
- Climax / Subplot dilemma *(sometimes)*
- Denouement

Act 3: Pay off the plot with the climax and resolution

- Exposition
- Inciting Incident
- Rising Action
- Dilemma
- **Core Climax**
- **Core Denouement** / Subplot Climax and Denouement

In the three-act structure, subplots usually, but not always, begin right at the second act, like we see marked above and underlined. They often progress quickly in the inciting incident and rising action.

Then, in the climactic moment of act two, just when you think everything should go well, a giant question mark is thrown into them.

In a love story subplot, this is often when we wonder *whether* the couple will actually get together in the end. Can they get past the things that are keeping them apart and finally connect?

In an adventure subplot, this might be a major setback,

when you wonder whether the goal the characters are working toward will ever be achieved.

Whatever happens, the subplot, which seemed to be going so strong, all of a sudden stops dead, and the audience is left to forget about it for a while.

The subplot might come back briefly here and there through to the third act, but it's usually not resolved until the final scene, one of the *most* effective moments to bring things together, when the subplot has its climactic moment and final denouement and resolution.

The above is just an example, and subplots find their ways in many other shapes and sizes. However, this can be a good general template for using a subplot in your story.

Use Subplots to Fill In Your Story

A great subplot will not save your lagging story. For a story to work, both the core plot *and* subplot must be working together to draw the reader through the rises and falls in the values of the story arc.

However, even the best stories can feel somewhat empty in the middle act alone. After all, it's easy for an author to run out of ideas, and for the characters to run out of drama to create.

Instead, fill that space with a subplot, and let it carry the burden of the middle of your story.

Key Ideas

- While stories have one main plot, they also can have subplots and internal plots which support the main plot.
- Most novels and films have two or three plots.
- The most common subplot type is a love story.

Practice

Subplot Exercise: Analyze three of your favorite novels or films. What is the main plot of each? What is the subplot, if it has one?

6
STORY ARCS: THE 6 SHAPES OF STORIES

In life, it can feel like things happen randomly, without causation, and with little or no meaning.

The human brain, though, *needs* meaning. We need to understand *why* things are going badly for us so we can avoid it or *why* things are going so well so we can do more of whatever's working.

This is why humans love story, because stories give us a sense of purpose, meaning, and shape. They do that through story arcs.

In stories, we get to see the cause-and-effect connections between otherwise random events. We get to experience the deeper meaning in life. We get to see through the chaos of real life and see the underlying pattern.

The literary term for this pattern is story arc, and humans *love* story arcs.

In this chapter, we're going to talk about the definition of story arcs, look at the six most commonly found story arcs in literature, talk about how to use them in your writing, and, finally, study which story arcs are the most successful.

Story Arc Definition

A story arc, or narrative arc, describes the shape of the change in value, whether rise or fall, over the course of the story.

Stories Rise and Fall in Arc Shapes

Stories change. If there is no rise or fall in a narrative, it isn't a story. It's a series of events.

The rise and fall of characters' fortunes interest us more than anything else.

This change, the rise and fall in a story, can be plotted on a graph to form a curve-shaped line.

And when you graph them, you begin to see patterns across all forms of story.

Here is a simple graph of a dramatic arc that Kurt Vonnnegut describes as "Man in a Hole":

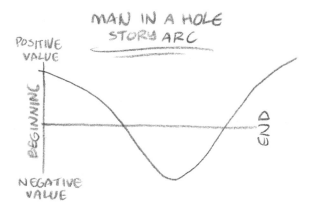

The x-axis of the graph describes the chronology of the narrative and the y-axis describes the positive or negative value the main character experiences.

That means that story arcs can also be character arcs, illustrating the character development that occurs throughout the plot.

However, while all character arcs are story arcs, not ALL story arcs are character arcs. In other words, some story arcs illustrate things separate from the main character's development, which we'll talk more about in the section "Story Arcs Measure Values" below.

The 6 Primary Story Arcs

Story arcs, of course, do not always follow such simple graphs. In fact, story arcs can often look more like this than a smooth curve:

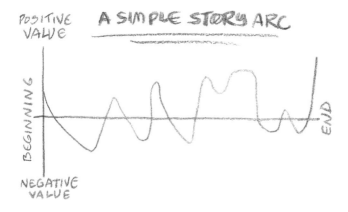

Yes, stories must change, but that doesn't mean they all change in the same ways.

But when you compare the story arcs of the best stories throughout history, patterns begin to emerge, and you find that these arcs are much more uniform than you might think.

That's what Andrew Reagan and his team of researchers

from the University of Vermont found after analyzing over 4,000 of the best novels from the Project Gutenberg library.

In fact they found that stories fall into six primary arcs.[1] Let's explore each one.

1. Rags to Riches (Rise)

All stories move, but some stories only have one movement.

In the Rags to Riches story arc, that movement is a continuous upward climb toward a happily ever after.

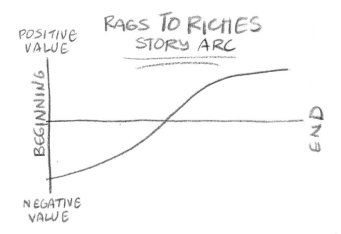

Examples of Rags to Riches story arcs:

- *Tangled* (Disney film)
- *The Winter's Tale* by William Shakespeare
- *Pride and Prejudice* by Jane Austen
- *Matilda* by Roald Dahl
- *Holes* by Louis Sachar
- *The BFG* by Roald Dahl

- *My Fair Lady* (film) / *Pygmalion* (novel) by George Bernard Shaw
- The Great American Dream / Progress

The Rags to Riches story arc is one of the most common story types, but these stories lag in popularity, according to Reagan, the researcher from the University of Vermont, who found that other arcs were more widely read.

2. Riches to Rags (Fall)

As with Rags to Riches, in a Riches to Rags story, there is just one movement. However, this movement is in the opposite direction, a *fall* rather than a rise.

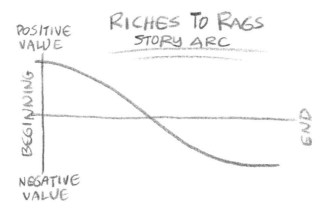

Examples of Riches to Rags story arcs:

- *Catcher in the Rye* by J.D. Salinger
- *Animal Farm* by George Orwell
- *Catch-22* by Joseph Heller

- *Love You Forever* by Robert Munsch
- *The Picture of Dorian Gray* by Oscar Wilde

In a Riches to Rags story, the protagonist begins the plot in a fairly high place, but slowly their life devolves until by the end, their life is a ruin of its former self.

Often, addiction stories or stories about mental health fit into this structure.

3. Man in a Hole (Fall Then Rise)

This is one of the most common and highly rated arcs, and is even an arc I used in my book *Crowdsourcing Paris*.

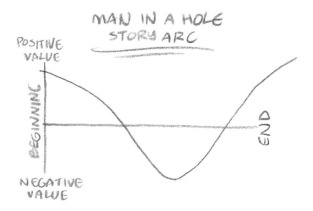

Examples of Man in a Hole story arcs:

- *The Hobbit* by J.R.R. Tolkien
- *Alice in Wonderland* by Lewis Carroll
- *Monsters, Inc.* (Disney film)
- *Finding Nemo* (Disney film)
- "Make America Great Again," Donald Trump's

Campaign Slogan

Many stories actually include two sequential Man in a Hole story arcs, as illustrated by this curve:

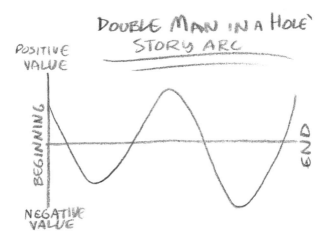

According to Reagan and the researchers at the University of Vermont, this is one of the most popular structures, and *the* most popular arc with a happy ending. He says in his paper:

"We find 'Icarus' (-SV 2), 'Oedipus' (-SV 3), and two sequential 'Man in a hole' arcs (SV 4), are the three most successful emotional arcs."

Examples of the Double Man in a Hole arc include:

- *Harry Potter and the Prisoner of Azkaban* by J.K. Rowling
- *The Lion King* (Disney film)
- And more

Some stories even contain many Man in a Hole arcs—

becoming Man in a Hole, Man in a Hole, Man in a Hole *ad infinitum*. *Lord of the Rings* and the 6,700-page online serialized novel *Worm* are examples of this.

4. Icarus / Freytag's Pyramid (Rise Then Fall)

This is the plot structure Gustav Freytag was interested in when he coined the plot structure now known as Freytag's Pyramid.

Contrary to popular belief, Freytag's Pyramid is *not* a universal structure for plot, but a description of a single arc.

For more on Freytag's Pyramid, and how it's been largely misunderstood, see the appendix.

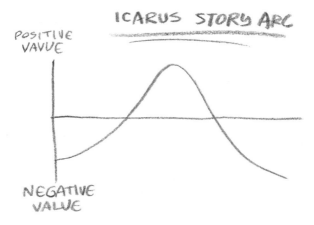

The Icarus arc, named after the Greek story about a boy who escapes imprisonment on an island by constructing wings made of wax but who ultimately falls into the sea after flying too close to the sun, is one of the most popular story arcs.

Examples of the Icarus story arc include:

- *Hunger Games* by Suzanne Collins
- *Macbeth* by William Shakespeare
- *Peter Pan*
- *The Old Man and the Sea / A Farewell to Arms* by Ernest Hemingway
- *The Fault in Our Stars* by John Green
- *Jurassic Park* by Michael Crichton
- *Titanic* (film)
- *Great Expectations* by Charles Dickens
- *The Great Gatsby* by F. Scott Fitzgerald
- *The Great Santini* by Pat Conroy

Apparently, if the word "great" is in the title, you know you're in for a sad ending! This is a popular story structure with literary writers, and tends to be a staple structure for many classics.

5. Cinderella (Rise Then Fall Then Rise)

The Cinderella arc, like Rags to Riches, is one of the *most* common arcs, often found in love stories, sports stories, Disney movies, and other stories with happy endings.

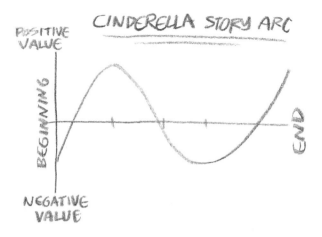

Examples of Cinderella story arcs:

- *Frozen* (Disney film)
- *Up* (Disney film)
- *How to Train Your Dragon* (film/novel)
- *Jane Eyre* by Emily Brontë
- *Pinocchio* (Disney film)
- *Aladdin* (Disney film)

If you're writing a Disney movie, there's a good chance it's going to be a Cinderella arc.

This is also commonly the arc of stories that follow **the Hero's Journey**. While the hero's journey can be more complicated than a single arc, most fit the Cinderella arc.

6. Oedipus (Fall Then Rise Then Fall)

The Oedipus arc is one of the most difficult structures to pull off, but it's also one of the most highly read structures.

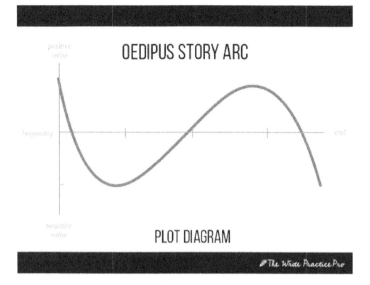

Examples of the Oedipus story arc include:

- *Moby Dick* by Herman Melville
- *Frankenstein* by Mary Shelley
- *And Then There Were None* by Agatha Christie
- *Lolita* by Vladimir Nabakov
- *The Sun Also Rises* by Ernest Hemingway
- *Gone with the Wind* by Margaret Mitchell
- *The Godfather* by Mario Puzo
- *Gone Girl* by Gillian Flynn
- *Hamlet* by William Shakespeare

How Story Arcs Fit Dramatic Structure

Dramatic structure describes the elements of a story's movement, and each of the above story arcs incorporates the dramatic structure.

Here's how these elements of dramatic structure fit into the Rags to Riches story arc:

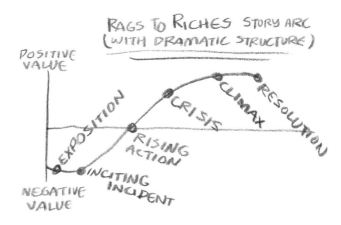

In this arc, the **exposition** has little to no movement and is primarily to acclimate the reader to the world of the story and its characters.

The **inciting incident** begins the upward movement.

The **rising action** describes the upward motion of the movement.

The combination of the **dilemma**, where the character must make a critical choice, and the **climax**, the moment of highest conflict and action, is the point of the peak, the make-or-break moment when things could either continue to improve or reverse.

Last, the **denouement** or **resolution** wraps up the plot at the end of the story with one or two scenes of relative stability. Denouement means untying in French, and in these final moments, the loose ends of the plot are tied up.

These components of dramatic structure can be found in every arc, and are part of what gives each arc their structure.

Story Arcs Can Also Fit Three-Act Structure

The three-act structure combines perfectly with story arcs, allowing flexibility in terms of the arc you're trying to create while also providing a structure that flows with the reader's expectations.

While this is not a law, commonly twenty-five percent of the arc is in the first act, fifty percent is in the second act, and the rest of the story fits into the final twenty-five percent, the final act.

More complicated arcs may actually have nine acts, or in other words, three three-act structures. Longer series or epics, stories with arcs that combine to form more complicated patterns, may even have twelve, eighteen, or even twenty-seven acts.

Story Arcs Measure Values

A story's rise and fall in value can be expressed generally in terms of "fortune," but you can also get more specific by measuring a story's movement based on the six story value scales.

For example, in an adventure story with a Man in a Hole arc set in space like the film *Gravity*, where the core value is physiological survival, you would measure the arc based on this life vs. death metric.

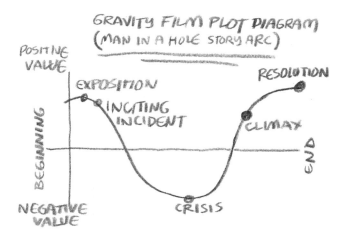

Let's break this arc down, analyzing the rise and fall of the life vs. death value throughout the key moments in the story:

Spoiler Alert

Exposition: Dr. Ryan Stone (Sandra Bullock) and astronaut Matt Kowalksi (George Clooney) are on a space walk on the Hubble Space Telescope. **Life vs. Death value measure:** stable.

Inciting Incident: A missile strike causes a chain reaction of space debris that threatens to destroy much of the spacecraft around the planet. **Life vs. Death value measure:** a threat of death appears.

Rising action: The space debris field begins to destroy spacecraft, including Stone and Kowalski's ship, and they have to escape to the International Space Station. But the spacecraft ISS has been damaged, and they have to travel to the Chinese space station. While en route, Kowalski sacrifices his life to save Stone. Other space shenanigans happen until Stone is out of options for survival. **Life vs. Death value measure:** inching closer and closer toward likely death.

Dilemma: As the sole survivor of the debris field and trapped in a Soyuz capsule without fuel, Stone has to choose whether to end her life or keep working to survive. Initially, she decides to turn off life support, but as she is losing consciousness, a vision of Kowalski gives her a final solution to reach the working Chinese reentry capsule. **Life vs. Death value measure:** near death.

Climax: Stone reaches the Chinese reentry capsule just as the space station is about to crash into the atmosphere. She unlocks from the station and is descending to Earth when a fire starts. After she lands safely in a lake, she has to evacuate the capsule immediately because of the smoke and nearly drowns before finally swimming to shore. **Life vs. Death value measure:** near death but survival becoming a slim possibility.

Denouement: Stone takes her first steps on Earth, thanking Kowalski, and as she watches the debris burn in Earth's atmosphere, a helicopter flies overhead, signaling her rescue. **Life vs. Death value measure:** survival by a small margin!

End Spoiler Alert

Notice how the story moves from *virtually no chance of death* to *death almost a certainty* to *the resolution*, where survival seems even more precious because of how close the protagonist came to death.

The story moves the value from the positive form to the negative, and depending on the value, back again. The story's arc is created through this rise and fall movement.

This same arc can be used to tell a love story, a performance story, or even a coming-of-age story. The arc stays the same, but the value being represented by the arc changes.

Can You Have Multiple Story Arcs?

Yes! In fact, most stories have multiple arcs.

Most novels and films are made by combining three plots and three different value scales like those listed above:

1. Main plot
2. Internal plot
3. Subplot

Here's the key point:

Each plot must have its own arc.

That means if you're writing an adventure story with a coming-of-age internal plot and a love story subplot—like *The Alchemist*, a quarter of the *Harry Potter* series, *A Tale of Two Cities*, or *The Da Vinci Code*—then you will have three different arcs, one for each plot.

The number of arcs you can include in your story depends on the scope of the story. Smaller stories have fewer arcs, and more complicated stories may have many arcs.

Short stories only have one arc. If you're writing a short story, it only has one arc. And usually that arc will only have one or two movements.

Sometimes, there are separate character arcs for each POV character. If you have multiple point of view characters or protagonists, you *may* have multiple story arcs, one for each character.

This is one reason to *avoid* having multiple protagonists, because it complicates the story, sometimes creating more arcs than you the writer (and your readers!) can keep track of, especially if you're relatively inexperienced.

Epics, novel or film series, and episodic stories have many arcs.

Soap operas, for example, often have so many arcs going that if you find yourself in the middle of a random episode it will feel extremely chaotic.

Often, episodic TV series will have one or two long arcs that last the whole series, while each episode has two or three smaller arcs.

Sitcoms, according to television writer Noah Charney,[2] often follow this structure:

- Teaser (exposition)—one to three minutes
- Trouble: Story A (inciting incident)—minute three
- Trouble: Story B (inciting incident)—minute six
- The Muddle: Story A (rising action, dilemma)—minute nine
- The Muddle: Story B (rising action, dilemma)—minute twelve
- The Triumph/Failure: Story A (climax)—minute thirteen
- The Triumph/Failure: Story B (climax)—minute fifteen
- The Kicker: Story A + B (denouement)—minute nineteen

In sitcoms, these two or three (when a C story is involved) arcs are usually independent from the overall arc of the series. However, occasionally, one or both of these arcs involve a longer running master arc of the show, carrying on plots that have been previously established.

A big reason for this is because unlike in novels, we don't want our favorite characters in sitcoms to change that much from episode to episode. While main characters like Sheldon in *The Big Bang Theory* do undergo character transformation in the series, their major quirks remain consistent episode to episode.

This also provides more opportunities for main characters to frequently fail as they attempt to achieve their episode goal, which provides more opportunities to drop jokes that pull at the character's steadfast personality traits and flaws.

Likewise, the Ross and Rachel arc from the sitcom *Friends* contains many movements over hundreds of episodes built up in ten years, but it is all done in one arc, usually using the same structure as the one above.

How to Use Story Arcs in Your Writing: 6 Writing Tips

Now that you understand the six main arcs and how the shapes of stories interact with a story's core value, how do you actually use this information to write great stories?

Here are six writing tips for using story arcs in your writing:

1. Above all, make sure your story moves.

It can move up, it can move down, it can move up and then down. But it *must* move, and that movement must begin *early*.

A narrative that stays the same is not a story but an account of events.

2. In the first draft, don't worry about matching your story to a particular arc.

You *might* know what your arc is when you start writing, and you might not.

Don't worry too much about it. Instead, tell your story (and make sure that story moves).

Don't get me wrong: you *can* use these arcs as templates, especially if your story idea is somewhat formless right now. But if you have a clear idea of your story, don't worry too much about whether it matches the arcs above.

3. In the first draft, do worry about finding your core value.

While you don't need to worry about finding the right shape of your story when you start writing, you *should* try to discover the core value, the y-axis that your story will move on.

If you can discover your core value (see the list of six values above for the options), you will be much more equipped to make sure it moves the way it needs to.

And while you *may* choose more than one value—perhaps a value for a subplot or the internal genre—if you try to move your story on too many values it will become muddied and will be very hard to work with in your second draft.

Above all, keep it simple. You can always write another book, but a book that's trying to do too much can easily become unworkable.

4. Know your genre and form and consider your arcs accordingly.

Different forms have different arc conventions.

As we explored above, most novels and films have three arcs, most sitcoms have two arcs, and most short stories have just one arc.

Genres have different conventions as well. Fantasy stories and romance stories often follow the Cinderella arc. Science fiction stories often use the Double Man in a Hole arc. Literary novels often use the Oedipus arc.

Study your genre and form to know which arcs are most common. If you find that they're commonly using one specific arc, it doesn't mean you're forced to use it too. But it *should* inform how you approach your arc choices, even if you decide to use a different one.

5. Write toward the dilemma.

When you're writing a first draft, you don't need to know everything that's going to happen.

If you're a pantser rather than a plotter, you might not know *anything* that happens.

But the best thing you can do is to write toward the dilemma.

The dilemma is the primary turning point in a story. It is

the moment when a character is presented with a difficult choice that will determine his or her fate.

This moment is usually found at the very bottom of a dip in a story arc or the very top of a peak. It will be followed almost immediately by the climax.

If you can find that dilemma, you will have found your story.

Everything in a story builds to the dilemma.

6. In your second draft, find each arc and enhance it.

While you don't need to know the shape of your main story arc or sub-arcs in your first draft, after you finish your first draft and before you start your second draft, find your arc.

What is its shape? How does it rise and fall? Does it fall enough? Does it rise enough? Is there enough movement?

The purpose of the second draft is to enhance your arc, to make it more pronounced, smoother and more effective.

How This Differs from Other Story Structure Frameworks

If you look at other frameworks for understanding story, like *The Seven Basic Plots*, *Save the Cat*, *The Plot Whisperer*, *Story Engineering*, and Freytag's Pyramid, you find that they are not talking about *all* plots (even if the authors think they are), but just specific story arcs.

For example, Freytag's Pyramid is about the Icarus arc, *The Seven Basic Plots* and *The Plot Whisperer* are essentially the Cinderella arc, and *Story Engineering* is Man in a Hole.

These frameworks make the claim that all stories follow the same arc. It's not true.

The reality is that story structure in general is *much* more flexible. In fact, plot type has *nothing* to do with story structure. You can have *any* shape of story, moving on *any* value scale.

For example, while the "standard" love story is a Cinderella arc, you can have a Man in a Hole love story arc like *Crazy Rich Asians* or an Oedipus arc like *The Breakup*.

The same is true for all the other plot types. You can find coming-of-age plots that follow each of these six arcs. Same with mystery plots, horror plots, and adventure plots.

Then, when you add in subplots and internal plots, you can create an infinite number of combinations, all based on the same six shapes.

That's what makes the Write Structure process so helpful. It's not "one size fits all." You can use it to better understand *any* kind of story that you want to tell.

All Good Stories Have an Arc

Good stories are about change, so all good stories have an arc.

By finding the arc in your story and making your story better, you can give your readers what they want: meaning.

All humans need meaning. While the world often can feel confusing, chaotic, and meaningless, the role of the storyteller is to help people find the meaning in their lives.

This is why humans love story.

And soon, it's why readers will love *your* story.

Key Ideas

- Good stories rise and fall in arc shapes.
- There are six main shapes that stories follow: Rags to Riches, Riches to Rags, Man in a Hole, Icarus, Cinderella, and Oedipus.
- Best-selling stories come in all shapes, but the three most common are double Man in a Hole, Icarus, and Oedipus.
- A story's main plot, subplot, and internal plot each have their own arc, allowing infinite combinations.
- Each storytelling form has its own arc conventions.

Novels and films tend to have three arcs. Sitcoms have two. Short stories have one.

Practice

Story Arc Exercise:

1. Choose one of the six story arcs: Rags to Riches, Riches to Rags, Man in a Hole, Icarus, Cinderella, or Oedipus.
2. Write a six-sentence story based on that arc.
3. Then, set your timer for fifteen minutes and expand your six-sentence story as much as you can.

PART III

ELEMENTS OF PLOT

To make a plot work, six elements that structure the story's movement must occur, and until you master these elements, you won't be able to develop better stories or hone your craft.

These six elements, explained fully in this chapter, are the following:

1. Exposition
2. Inciting Incident
3. Rising Action
4. Dilemma
5. Climax
6. Denouement

Do you want readers to love your story?

Then you need to understand how to apply the six elements that structure a plot.

7
ELEMENT 1: EXPOSITION

At the beginning of the story, the exposition establishes characters and setting. Not all your world-building happens here, but this is where you show your readers what "normal" is for your characters. That way, readers will know what's wrong when we hit the next step. If we don't understand a character's status quo—if we don't spend any time getting to know *them*—we won't have much reason to root for them when their normal life gets tossed off course.

Take a look at the definition for exposition for a more literal idea of its function in a plot.

Exposition Definition

> The exposition is a set of scenes in a story meant to introduce the audience to the characters, world, and tone of the story. It is relatively short, and no major changes occur.

Where Exposition Fits in the Dramatic Structure

In dramatic structure, the exposition occurs at the beginning of the story. It is the first element in the list of six, and it is meant to set up the inciting incident, which is a moment where the action kicks off in the plot.

How Long Are Most Expositions?

Since stories are about change and values in conflict, the exposition, which contains no change, is necessarily quite short.

Most expositions are just two or three scenes, and sometimes they are just half a scene.

For example, in *The Hobbit*, there are just a couple of pages of exposition before Gandalf shows up and invites Bilbo on an adventure.

Here are a few more examples of expositions in literature:

Romeo and Juliet

In *Romeo and Juliet*, the exposition is actually quite long, even longer depending on where you put the inciting incident (Freytag puts it earlier than I would, but then, Freytag has a different way of thinking about story structure):

- Servants of the two leading families in the city, the Montagues and Capulets, feud in the streets
- Romeo, a young son of the Montagues, is depressed after being rejected by a woman and his friends attempt to cheer him up
- Juliet, the daughter of the Capulets, chafes at her parents setting her up with a man
- Romeo's friends convince him to attend a party at the Capulets

At this party, Romeo meets Juliet, and falls in love at first sight, creating the inciting incident. It is then that the main action of the play begins.

But it isn't until the fifth scene that this inciting incident occurs, which makes this one of the longer expositions.

Note: Gustav Freytag argues that the invitation to the Capulet's party is actually the inciting incident, which would make the exposition a bit shorter, just three scenes. I get this, from a certain perspective, since it's the party that throws the two families together irrevocably, but I think that event is dwarfed by instant attraction between the two lovers.

Exposition Length: four scenes

Gravity

In contrast, the film *Gravity*, which we examined in detail in Chapter 6, has an exposition that is quite short.

The inciting incident—the missile strike that causes a chain reaction of space debris—occurs at the end of the first scene, meaning the exposition is less than a scene long.

Length: less than one scene

Now that you know what an exposition is and how it fits into a story, how do you write one that's good? This is especially important considering the exposition is both the first part of your story *and* the part with the least action.

With that in mind, here are six tips to help you write a great exposition:

1. Begin With Your Story's Core Value

As we talked about in our discussion of story arcs in Chapter 6, every story has a core value scale that it moves on, and when you begin a story, your very first scene should be about the core value of your story.

To recap, these are the traditional six value scales:

1. Life vs. Death
2. Life vs. a Fate *Worse* than Death
3. Love vs. Hate
4. Accomplishment vs. Failure
5. Maturity vs. Naïveté
6. Good vs. Evil

Stories rise and fall on the scale of these values. A love story might begin in the middle of the love vs. hate scale, rise during the meet cute, fall during a break up, and end high on the love scale.

In your exposition, part of your job is to establish what scale your story is moving on. Your story may play with several of these values, but whatever your *core* value is must be presented from the very first scene.

Are you telling an adventure story on the life vs. death scale? Then begin with your first life vs. death moment.

Are you telling a performance story about a team competing to win a major tournament? Then begin with a scene that deals with accomplishment and failure.

Are you telling a story about good and evil? Show the audience a moment when good confronts evil right at the start.

Your exposition is not just about introducing your setting and characters. It's also about introducing the values at play in your story.

When you start with these values and keep them in mind throughout the rest of your story, you'll find the story comes together.

2. Just Because There's No Major Change Doesn't Mean There's No Conflict or Choice

Stories can feel slow and boring during the exposition, even when they're by great authors. Worse, they can drag when authors make the mistake of using exposition to introduce characters, provide backstory, and develop their world without any real advancement, caused by change, in the plot.

Avoid this.

Despite the exposition's role in establishing a character's status quo, it's still part of the story, and all story relies on conflict and choice to create plot advancement.

Without movement in a plot, readers will read five pages of a story and put it down. They'll be bored because nothing significant happens.

Instead, incorporate the six elements into a scene, just as you use them to build your dramatic structure.

It is these six elements within every scene that will keep your story moving.

That means every *scene*, even a scene in the exposition, must have an exposition, an inciting incident, a rising action, a dilemma, a climax, and a denouement.

For example, let's look back at the opening scene in *Romeo and Juliet*, in which the servants from the Montagues and Capulets feud on the streets.

We could outline the scene like this:

1. **Exposition:** Two Capulet servants talk about their hatred of the Montagues.
2. **Inciting Incident:** Two Montague servants come onstage and a verbal feud begins.
3. **Rising Complication:** Benvolio, a Montague, tries to stop the fight, but Tybalt, a Capulet, insults him.
4. **Dilemma:** Benvolio must choose whether to fight and break the peace or to allow himself to be called a coward.
5. **Climax:** Tybalt and Benvolio fight until their fight is broken up by armed citizens.
6. **Denouement:** The Prince declares that anyone who breaks the peace will be executed.

See how, even though this is just a scene in the exposition, it still contains all the elements of dramatic structure?

So, too, any scene in *your* exposition should have this dramatic structure, or else risk feeling like boring info-dumping.

3. Introduce Your Characters

While you can introduce characters throughout the first act of your story (it's usually not a good idea to introduce them afterward), it's your exposition's job to introduce *most* of your cast.

This is a lesson I learned the hard way in my memoir, *Crowdsourcing Paris*, when I introduced a pivotal character all the way at the end of act two.

When a beta reader gave me feedback that I needed to introduce the character earlier, I did a massive facepalm. I should have known better!

So I moved up the character's introduction, and it made the story flow much better.

Aim to introduce most of your major characters in the exposition.

4. Save the Cat

One tried-and-true method of introducing a central character in the best possible light is to have them "save the cat." This is a screenwriting term popularized by Blake Snyder in his book of the same name, and it refers to a character who does a selfless, or at least admirable, act to prove they are "worth rooting for." The result is that it endears them to the reader early on in the story.

The term comes from *Roxeanne*, the 1987 film starring Steve Martin and Darryl Hannah, in which Martin, who has a strangely long nose, literally saves a cat from a tree at the beginning of the film. The intent for this action is to ensure the audience loves him despite his strange appearance.

This admirable act, of course, does *not* have to be saving a cat. Here are some examples of this device in popular stories:

- *Aladdin*: After stealing a loaf of bread and escaping the police, Aladdin offers his share to two hungry-looking children, proving that he's a thief with character.
- *Harry Potter and the Sorcerer's Stone*: If being an orphan who is bullied by the uncle, aunt, and cousin he lives with isn't enough for readers to bond with Harry, he also befriends and then saves a snake from a humiliating captivity. (Save the snake is a less catchy guideline, but it works!)
- *Pride and Prejudice*: Elizabeth Bennet is first singled out as worth rooting for by her father, when he compares her to her sisters, saying, "Lizzy has something more of quickness than her sisters." Then later, we cheer for her when she's insulted by Mr. Darcy and instead of getting angry, she laughs it off.
- *The Hobbit*: Bilbo Baggins, like many of us, both longs for adventure (because of his Took ancestry, as Tolkien explains) and is very uncomfortable about it. This inner turmoil makes him the perfect "everyman" hero thrown into the midst of a very tumultuous situation involving dwarves and dragons. He is like us, and we always want to root for ourselves.

While a selfless or admirable act is not required, it is important to somehow develop a bond with your characters early on, and this technique is one of the best, most efficient ways to do it.

5. Build to the Inciting Incident Quickly

As we showed in our examples, the exposition isn't meant to be long: as short as half a scene and as long as four.

The point here is to get to the point: the inciting incident.

The inciting incident is when the story will begin moving, and a story that doesn't move doesn't make for a good story. More on this in the next element.

Overall, don't dawdle. Do what you need to do to set up the inciting incident, and then move on.

6. Some Books Don't Start With the Exposition

In some stories, especially action, thriller, or horror stories, it's appropriate to begin with a short scene of heightened tension. There are several ways to handle this:

In medias res, meaning "in the middle" in Latin, is a literary technique to start a story in the middle of the action. This begins the story with a heightened level of suspense at the expense of clarity for the sake of the reader. The audience, who don't know the characters caught in the action, can easily feel distant or confused when stories start this way.

However, in certain stories and genres this is well worth it for the sake of an immediate shot of action. A good example of a story that starts *in medias res* is almost every film in the Mission Impossible franchise, allowing the story to begin with an immediate shot of adrenaline.

Flash-forward. Similarly, a story that starts with a flash-forward (as opposed to a flashback) begins not in the exposition, but in the climax—not a full climax but a shortened glimpse of the climax. Then, in the middle of the dilemma of the scene, you pull away from the scene and flash back to the start of the story, the exposition. A good example of this technique is *Fight Club* by Chuck Palahniuk (both the novel and film versions).

There are drawbacks to beginning with a moment deep in the action of the story. You can miss the opportunity to build a bond between your audience and your characters. You also risk confusing and disorienting them.

The writers who do it the best draw the audience as quickly out of the action as they drew them in, soon beginning a normal exposition.

However, even for stories that don't begin with it, the exposition is a necessary part of any story's structure, and if you omit it, you'll leave your reader feeling lost and listless later. What is always true of successful stories is that you have to get through the exposition at *some* point, even if it's not the first scene.

Good Stories Start With Clear Choices

If you want to write a great story, you don't start too fast with a climactic moment. You also don't start too slow with no choices or conflict.

Instead, start with a strong exposition by using events that force your main characters into important choices, ones that will end in inevitable consequences. By focusing on forcing choices instead of using too much description, you're calling your main characters to act.

And when a character acts, they're simultaneously developed along with the plot, instead of separated from it.

Key Ideas

- The exposition is the first element in the six elements of a plot. Here, a scene or more is used to introduce the reader to the characters, world, and tone of the story.
- Most expositions are just two or three scenes, and sometimes they are just half a scene.
- When you begin a story, your very first scene should be about the core value of your story.

- Even though it occurs in the story's beginning, exposition still needs to have conflict.
- Your exposition should introduce most of your cast.
- Include a save the cat moment in your exposition.
- Use the exposition to set up your inciting incident, and get to this quickly.
- Some stories don't start with an exposition. These are books that start *in medias res*.

Practice

Story Analysis Exercise: Find your favorite movie or book and, for fifteen minutes, watch the movie or read the first scenes in the book. How many scenes does it take to get to an inciting incident—when the status quo is thrown off course? What were the exposition scenes before it and how did they develop the cast, world, and time? Reflect on this briefly in a journal.

Writing Practice Exercise: For ten minutes, journal about the main characters, world, and time for your story. Then, spend five minutes writing one or two sentences that describe the exposition/beginning scene(s) establishing this. Make sure that there is a clear *conflict* in this description!

Example: After a quick prologue that shows Jafar's failed attempt to get into the Cave of Wonders, Aladdin, Agraba's street rat, steals a loaf of bread with his best friend, the monkey Abu. They escape the police, but Aladdin offers his share to two hungry-looking children, proving that he's a thief with character.

8

ELEMENT 2: INCITING INCIDENT

You might have heard that you need to start a story with a bang, that you need to begin with deep conflict. Or perhaps you've heard literary agents say they want to be hooked by a story in the first few pages.

In the beginning of stories or scenes, such hooks are created by the inciting incident.

This event creates the first significant moment in the core plot; it's when the main character is thrown into a challenging situation that upsets the status quo.

Whether the inciting incident is coincidental or caused by another character, it will officially begin the story arc, either in a positive way or negative, and this movement will culminate in the climax and denouement, the last two elements of plot. (More to come!)

Understanding the definition of the inciting incident and how it works in a story is crucial for you to write your own story that moves with urgency.

Inciting Incident Definition

The inciting incident is an event in a story that upsets the status quo and begins the story's movement, either in a positive way or negative, that culminates in the climax and denouement.

Criteria for an Inciting Incident

Inciting incidents have four criteria:

1. **Interruption:** Inciting incidents are an interruption in the character's normal life.
2. **Out of the protagonist's control:** Inciting incidents are not caused by the character and are not a result of the character's desires.
3. **Urgent:** Inciting incidents necessitate urgent action.
4. **Early:** Inciting incidents happen early in the story, sometimes in the first scene, often within the first three to four scenes.

Other story structure frameworks call the inciting incident by different names, including the call to adventure (Campbell), the catalyst (Snyder), the hook (Wells), simply the problem (Miller), and my favorite, the exciting force (Freytag).

The only term I *don't* think is helpful is the hook, since it combines the inciting incident, which holds a structural place within every story, with the hook, a device to capture the reader's attention in the first pages of a story.

A good story might not have a hook and still work as a story, but without an inciting incident, a story won't move, and without movement it will cease being a story and become a series of events.

Let's talk more about what the inciting incident *is* and *is not*, but first, let's talk about how the inciting fits into the dramatic structure.

The Length of the Inciting Incident

The inciting incident, like all interruptions, can happen in as little as a moment, but it is usually set into one scene.

The Inciting Incident is More Than a Want or Need

Some story structure theorists say that the character's desire or need is enough for an inciting incident.

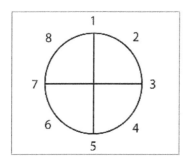

Dan Harmon, the screenwriter and creator of the show *Community*, founded a framework called the Story Circle theory. There are many things to like about this structure, which on the surface seems perfect for episodic stories like television sitcoms and also film series.

Here's how he describes the basic structure in a tutorial he wrote:

Draw a circle and divide it in half vertically.

Divide the circle again horizontally.

Starting from the twelve o'clock position and going clockwise, number the four points where the lines cross the circle 1, 3, 5, and 7.

Number the quarter sections themselves 2, 4, 6, and 8.

Here we go, down and dirty:

1. A character is in a zone of comfort,
2. But they want something.
3. They enter an unfamiliar situation,

4. Adapt to it,
5. Get what they wanted,
6. Pay a heavy price for it,
7. Then return to their familiar situation,
8. Having changed.

Did you spot the inciting incident in there?

"But they want something."

Donald Miller's definition of story in *A Million Miles in a Thousand Years* is "A character who wants something and is willing to go through conflict to get it."

Yes, desire is important in any story. It's just not the inciting incident.

According to 2011 interview in *Wired*[1], Dan Harmon apparently got the idea for this structure after watching and rewatching the film *Die Hard*.

But is that how *Die Hard* works? John McLane just *wanted* something? And he got it?

No, the story doesn't begin because of John's desires. It begins because of an **interruption**. Alan Rickman and his terrorist friends come in with guns and take everyone hostage. John may have *wanted* to be with his wife and patch up his marriage, but that's going to have to wait until the people who want to kill him are dealt with.

The inciting incident in *Die Hard* is an early, urgent interruption that is outside of the character's control.

Compare this to desires. Desires can become urgent. They can even interrupt you, but ultimately they are in your control, whether you take action on them or not.

Inciting Incidents Can Be Positive or Negative, But They Are Always Interruptions

Some story gurus call the inciting incident "the problem." (Miller, by the way, has since changed his definition of the inciting incident to "the problem," moving away from a character's desire.)

Others call it something more positive, "the call to adventure," for example.

These definitions contradict each other, because the truth is the inciting incident can be negative in some stories, a problem; or positive, an adventure, in others.

Often they are *both* positive *and* negative!

Some stories have negative inciting incidents. Like in *Die Hard*. For John McClane, the protagonist, that was hardly a positive thing.

Other stories have inciting incidents that are largely positive. In most love stories, the inciting incident takes the form of a "meet cute," a moment when the couple at the heart of the story first meet and have an emotional connection—which sometimes looks like attraction and sometimes hatred.

This is an example of a positive inciting incident, a happy interruption.

It is true that problems *always* result from the inciting incident, but inciting incidents don't always look like a problem at first. In fact, they can sometimes look like the best thing that ever happened to a character.

Inciting Incidents Are Tied to the Core Value in Your Story

As we've learned, different types of stories have, at their core, different values. The value at the core of a story will alter the inciting incident.

This sounds more complicated than it is.

A love story, with the core value scale of love vs. hate, will have an inciting incident that looks very different than a fantasy adventure story with the core value of life vs. death.

Those inciting incidents will look still different than a thriller with the core value of life vs. a fate *worse* than death.

10 Types of Inciting Incidents

As writers throughout history have told millions of stories, these inciting incidents have grown to find similar structures, and even have gotten names based on how they work.

Here are the ten types of inciting incidents, based on the six story values:

1. Call to Adventure/Death Plus MacGuffin (Action/Adventure Stories: Life vs. Death)

"This mission, should you choose to accept it," the self-destructing tape says.

For adventure and action stories, the protagonists are invited to some kind of adventure or mission.

Sometimes they are invited by a victim (in the case of Luke Skywalker), a mentor (in the case of Frodo), or a villain (in the case of Mr. Incredible).

The person doing the inviting matters less than the fact that an adventure or mission is beginning.

A final version of this inciting incident is the "Death Plus MacGuffin," when a minor character dies, leaving a clue or piece of a MacGuffin—which is a kind of talisman object that the protagonist has to hunt for over the course of the rest of the story.

Stories with this inciting incident include:

- *Crowdsourcing Paris* by J.H. Bunting (that's me)
- *Saving Private Ryan* (film)
- *The Lord of the Rings* by J.R.R. Tolkein
- *Mr. Incredible* (Disney film)
- Every *Star Wars* film
- And more!

2. Death of a Loved One/A Great Crime Against Me (Action/Adventure Stories: Life vs. Death)

An alternative to the direct call to adventure is the "death of a loved one" inciting incident, which spurs the protagonist to get revenge or find justice.

Stories that are primarily revenge plots have a version of this inciting incident. I call it "A Great Crime Against Me," in which some horrible act is done against the protagonist, forcing him or her to vow revenge.

Stories with this inciting incident include:

- *The Count of Monte Cristo* by Alexandre Dumas
- *Braveheart* (film)
- *Batman Begins* (film)
- *Kill Bill* (film)

3. Show Me the Body (Mystery/Crime/Thriller/Horror Story: Life vs. a Fate Worse than Death)

What's worse than death? Being brutally tortured and then murdered before you die.

That's what's at the heart of most thrillers, mysteries, and horror stories.

And nearly all of these stories, when they're done well, begin with the discovery of a dead body, kicking off the solution for the murder, or the hunt for/escape from the monster.

Stories with this inciting incident include:

- Every detective story ever
- *Jaws* (film)
- *Silence of the Lambs* by Thomas Harris

Occasionally, these types of stories don't start with a dead body but with some kind of mystery. Most Sherlock Holmes novels, for example, don't start with a body, but the structure remains the same.

4. The Haunted House/Forbidden Object

(Mystery/Crime/Thriller/Horror Story: Life vs. a Fate Worse than Death)

A type specific to horror stories is the "haunted house" or "forbidden object" inciting incident.

This is when the characters stumble upon something eerie, whether a place or an object, something they know they shouldn't interact with, but they choose to do it anyway (or are forced to).

This eerie thing can be a place, an object, or even a person.

Stories with this inciting incident include:

- *House* by Ted Dekker and Frank Peretti
- *Poltergeist* (film)
- *Locke & Key* (TV series)

5. Meet Cute (Love Story: Love vs. Hate)

The couple meets for the first time and an emotional connection is made. Often something embarrassing happens. Frequently, they hate each other.

Whatever happens, sparks fly.

Stories with this inciting incident include:

- *The Notebook* by Nicholas Sparks
- The subplot in *Frozen* (Disney film)
- Every Hollywood Romcom

6. Betrayal (Love Story: Love vs. Hate)

There are two types of love stories: one in which the couple gets together and the other in which the couple separates.

In the stories in which the couple separates, the inciting incident almost always includes some kind of betrayal, usually an infidelity.

Stories with this inciting incident include:

- *Kane vs. Kane* (film)
- *Betrayal* by Harold Pinter

Note: No one likes these stories, especially me, so that's why there are so few examples. Sorry!

7. The Tournament (Performance/Sports Story: Accomplishment vs. Failure)

In stories involving the performance of some skill or talent, or sports stories involving a sports team or individual, the inciting incident involves entry into some kind of tournament or competition.

Stories with this inciting incident include:

- *Miracle* (film)
- *Remember the Titans* (film)
- *Paper Lion* by George Plimpton

8. There be Dragons Here (Coming-of-Age Story: Maturity vs. Naïveté)

Coming-of-age stories often have an inciting incident involving something that is outside of the protagonist's current worldview.

Perhaps it's the existence of magic or the kindness of a stranger or an opportunity to enter a new social class.

Whatever it is, it throws the protagonist into confusion and shows them how little they understand the world.

Stories with this inciting incident include:

- *How to Train Your Dragon* (film/novel)
- *Great Expectations* by Charles Dickens

- *Harry Potter and the Sorcerer's Stone* by J.K. Rowling

Note: Since coming-of-age is rarely the *main* plot of a story, and is more often an internal plot, this will not usually be the main inciting incident.

9. Principal's Office (Coming-of-Age Story: Maturity vs. Naïveté)

Another approach to the coming-of-age story involves the character getting into trouble early on, often in a school setting. This forces the character to begin the process of reflecting on his or her life and making changes.

Stories with this inciting incident include:

- *Good Will Hunting* (film)
- *The Breakfast Club* (film)

10. The Temptation (Morality Story: Good vs. Evil)

In morality stories about the forces of good vs. evil, the inciting incident often involves some kind of temptation of the protagonist.

Stories with this inciting incident include:

- *The Dark Knight* (film)
- *Dr. Faustus* by Christopher Marlowe

The Inciting Incident Is Simple: Throw Rocks

Whenever the idea of trying to tell a story gets too complicated, I come back to this one simple piece of writing advice that's over a hundred years old. You might have heard it before. It goes:

In the first act, put your character up a tree. In the second act, throw rocks at them. In the third act, bring them down.

That's it. That's all you have to do in your inciting incident. Just put your character up a tree so they can be an easy target for rocks.

It's not complicated.

Don't get overwhelmed by all of the different types of inciting incidents or the terminology.

Just figure out how to put your character up a tree so that you can start throwing rocks.

Key Ideas

- The inciting incident is an event in a story that upsets the status quo and begins the story's movement, either in a positive way or negative, that culminates in the climax and denouement.
- Inciting incidents have four criteria: they interrupt the status quo, they're out of the protagonist's control, they're urgent, and they're early in the plot.
- The inciting incident is not synonymous with the hook.
- Desire needs to happen in every story, but it is not the same as the inciting incident—an inciting incident is an interruption.
- Inciting incidents can be positive or negative as long as they interrupt the status quo.
- Problems *always* result from the inciting incident, but inciting incidents don't always look like a problem at first.
- Inciting incidents are tied to the core value in your story.
- There are ten types of inciting incidents based on the six core values.

Practice

Story Analysis Exercise: Continue with the movie or book you chose for the exposition practice exercise. First, identify the story value for this story (life vs. death, love vs. hate, etc.). Then, spend five minutes journaling about the main character's status quo. Finally, take the next ten minutes to identify an interruption in this story that upsets the status quo and moves on the story's value. Reflect on this briefly in a journal.

Writing Practice Exercise: For five minutes, journal about the status quo for your story's main character. Then, spend ten minutes coming up with five possible interruptions that could uproot your main character's status quo and also move on your story's core value.

9

ELEMENT 3: RISING ACTION OR PROGRESSIVE COMPLICATIONS

If you've ever told a good story—one that has your friends or family on the floor laughing, or else on the edge of their seat asking, "What happened next?!"—then you know that you *can't* get to the point of the story too quickly.

Instead, you draw out interest. You talk about all the things that went wrong. You make jokes and accentuate the best details. When you're done, it's the punchline people remember, but it's everything leading up to it that makes the story *work*.

The same is true when you're writing a story, particularly in novels, memoirs, and screenplays. It's called the Rising Action, and it's essential to get it right IF you want to write entertaining, informative, and deeply connecting stories.

Not to mention, the rise in progressive complications—or obstacles a character faces as they move throughout the plot towards their story goal—is what increases tension. They're what make the climax of the story the moment we've all been waiting to see.

Reaching the top of Mount Everest wouldn't be nearly as impressive or rewarding (or interesting) if it were an *easy*, quick climb.

The spine of the story comes to life in the progressions.

Rising Action Definition

The rising action in a story is a series of events that move the plot toward the climax. To do this, it builds the action with a series of progressive complications, or events that create conflict by preventing a character from easily attaining their goals and desires. These obstacles escalate in intensity, leading to the dilemma. In fact, Robert McKee calls the rising action the "progressive complications" because the story gets more complicated as it progresses. As the source of the chief conflict, the rising action contains most of the action in a story, and is usually the longest element.

How the Rising Action Works in a Story

The **purpose** of the rising action is to lead the character to make a difficult decision.

However, most people, including most characters, are reluctant to make decisions, especially difficult ones that result in inevitable consequences for either themselves or others.

That's what the rising action is for, moving the characters to a point where they are *forced* to make *that* decision.

The rising action does this by putting the characters through a series of progressively more complicated events and choices.

Things get more and more complicated for the protagonist until they reach a turning point—that moment that thrusts the lead character of a scene into a decision that, whether they choose to act or not, ends with consequences (positive or negative).

That point of decision-making creates a dilemma for the character.

And this dilemma is always a choice between two conflicting values, whether safety or sacrifice, love or duty, performance or righteousness, etc.

The Rising Action Builds the Conflict Between Two Values

This conflict between two values and the protagonist's choice between them is what creates drama.

As we've discussed, stories need conflict. Conflict is what drives the plot. But effective stories are not driven by conflict for the sake of conflict. They're driven by conflict for the sake of forcing a *choice*.

In other words, it is the character's decisions that drive effective stories forward, not the events that the character is experiencing. Choice and events work together, with the latter creating an opportunity for the former—and the former is what calls a character to *act*.

In a moment, we'll look at several different examples. But first, I need to make one quick note about the different ways people talk about the rising action.

Freytag's Rising Action vs. Modern 3-Act Story Structure

Freytag's Pyramid is one of the most common frameworks for story structure. Formulated by Gustav Freytag in 1863, this concept, more than anything else, has shaped the way people think about story structure today.

That being said, Freytag's own understanding of plot and structure differs greatly from how most writers think and talk about it now.

Writers today include all the same elements as Freytag. But we put them in different places, as you'll see in the illustration below.

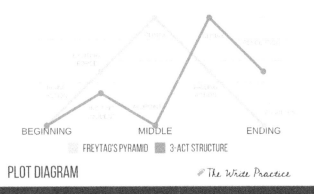

FREYTAG'S PYRAMID VS. TRADITIONAL 3 ACT STORY STRUCTURE

PLOT DIAGRAM — *The Write Practice*

While this illustration isn't perfectly to scale, if the rising action contains everything after the exposition and through to the climax, then, in Freytag's model, the rising action—which Freytag calls the rising movement—is significantly shorter than in a modern three-act story structure model.

Despite their differences, these models *can* overlap, and you can use both to better think through the structure of your story. I mention this mainly to clarify the language I use in the examples below.

Examples of Rising Action

Now let's look at examples of the rising action, rising movement, or progressive complications in action.

As we analyze them, let's begin with the choice each story builds toward. As I said above, the purpose of the rising action is to force a character into a choice because choices are the source of drama.

Thus, we will work backward from that decision, showing how the rising action forces that character into that decision.

Romeo and Juliet

Beginning with the dilemma, how does the rising action in *Romeo and Juliet* work?

The climactic choice/dilemma: end their lives OR stay alive in a world without the other.

Out of context, both of those decisions are crazy. Why would a young, newlywed couple decide to separate? Even more extreme, why would two young people with so much potential from good families decide to end their lives?

These decisions are the core of the story, the climactic moments. They are also decisions no one would come to without some good reason.

The rising action provides the reason. If we begin from that choice and work backward, we can see how the rising action builds to that dilemma.

The events in the rising action are:

- Romeo believes Juliet is dead.
- Juliet fakes her own death, but the message telling Romeo of her plan is never delivered.
- Juliet is forced to become engaged to another man (even though she's already married to Romeo).
- Romeo is exiled, and he and Juliet part tearfully.
- Romeo kills Tybalt, Juliet's cousin, after Tybalt kills Mercutio, Romeo's best friend.*
- Romeo and Juliet elope in secret.
- Romeo and Juliet meet at a party and fall in love, despite the fact that their families are enemies.
- **Exposition:** Two rival families fight in the streets of Verona.

*This is where Freytag marks the end of the rising movement, with the climax being Romeo and Juliet parting tearfully. Most modern three-act story structures would mark that scene as part of the rising action/progressive complications.

From this perspective, the choice makes perfect sense, and the stakes are well set up so that this choice is significantly difficult.

Climactic choices *must* be difficult. If they're not, the writer hasn't done their job correctly.

Also note, the rising action covers a lot of ground, a large majority of the story. Even if you end the rising action where Freytag does—and again, few writers today would do that—it still covers almost half of the play.

Let's look at another example, this one from *Ready Player One*.

Ready Player One

What is the dilemma, the climactic choice that Wade Watts, a.k.a. Parzival, has to make in *Ready Player One*?

First, a brief summary, in case you're not familiar with the story. In a dystopian future, Wade Watts spends most of his time in a virtual reality world called the OASIS. Halliday, the rich and famous creator of the OASIS, has died, and he's left an elaborate puzzle hidden in this virtual world to determine who will inherit his fortune and control of the OASIS. Wade stumbles upon the first clue, then races thousands of other hopeful puzzle solvers to win the game.

The climactic choice/dilemma: Go it alone OR share the winnings from the game with his friends.

The winnings in *Ready Player One* include billions of dollars plus full administrative control of the OASIS. It's everything Wade Watts has ever wanted. Why on earth would he even be tempted to share that?

The rising action gives us the answer. As with *Romeo and*

Juliet, if we begin from that choice and work backward, we can see how the rising action builds to that dilemma.

The events in the rising action of *Ready Player One* include most of the events in the story, from (spoiler alert!) the moment he shares the information about how to beat Joust and receive the first key with Art3mis up until (more spoilers) he hesitates before entering the final crystal gate and getting the chance to play to win Halliday's Easter egg.

Building up to that moment, Wade undergoes a personal transformation. He changes from someone who chooses, on principle, to do things alone to someone who has a few close friends—including a pseudo-girlfriend in Art3mis. Then he becomes someone who is once again alone and alienated from everyone he cares about, before ultimately becoming someone who is willing to risk it all and sacrifice for the sake of his friends.

As he goes through this maturation process, he learns the story of Halliday, a tragic model of someone who decided to alienate his friends for the sake of his creation, the OASIS.

Through the rising action, in other words, the choice becomes whether Wade will become like Halliday, his hero, or learn critical lessons from Halliday and share power with his friends.

The Rising Action Belongs In Each Act *and* Each Scene

Your story needs rising action, but so does every act and scene.

That means the average novel, film, or screenplay—which has fifty to seventy scenes—should have fifty to seventy rising actions and fifty to seventy climactic choices.

Why so many?

Because this is the heart of drama: complications creating conflict between values resulting in a choice. If you don't have progressively more difficult complications and if you don't have progressively more significant choices, you don't have a story.

So figure out the choices your characters need to make, and then build to them using the rising action.

Key Ideas

- The rising action moves the plot toward the climax. It does this by building the action with a series of progressive complications, or events that create conflict by preventing a character from easily attaining their scene or story want/goal.
- As the source of the chief conflict, the rising action contains most of the action in a story, and is usually the longest piece.
- The **purpose** of the rising action is to lead the character to make a difficult decision.
- Effective stories are not driven by conflict for the sake of conflict, but driven by conflict for the sake of forcing a *choice*. The choice should be between two values.
- Your story and every scene in it need rising action.

Practice

Story Analysis Exercise: Continue with the scene from the movie or book you chose for the last two exercises. First, if you haven't yet, find the inciting incident in that scene. Then, spend fifteen minutes listing obstacles, conflicts, and complications that build up the action of the scene.

Writing Practice Exercise: What value is your story turning on? Have you picked yet? If not, choose one of the main story values. Then, spend five minutes listing events that would push your main character up and down the value scale. Next to each event, write the value beside it with a positive or negative sign.

For example, if you were writing a love story with a value scale of love vs. hate, your list might look like this:

1. Two young people meet at a friend's dinner party (+Love)
2. But they instantly despise each other (-Hate)
3. But they're both best friends with the host and everyone else at the party are a couple so they have to spend the whole night together (-Hate)
4. Just when they're about to leave, there is a storm: the power goes out and the roads close so no one can leave (-Hate)
5. Stuck together, they see some attractive qualities in each other (+Love)
6. They accidentally kiss (+Love)
7. But then it's revealed one of them has a girlfriend, which causes the other to think they were cheating (-Hate)
8. But the girlfriend is the worst and they left a break up voicemail just before the party (+Love)
9. The power finally comes back on and the roads clear. They're about to leave.

And so on. You can see how as you play with the value scale, you can easily create complications for the characters that move them up or down the value scale. Give it a try!

10

ELEMENT 4: DILEMMA

As we've said, the dilemma is the most important of the six elements. A good example of the dilemma done well is the film *Gravity*, which we discussed in-depth in Chapter 6. Sandra Bullock's character's problem is that everything is trying to kill her. The progressive complications get worse and worse until everyone is dead except for her.

This is where many writers would stop. They would show her struggle to survive and resolve it by eventually getting to a place where she *does,* in fact, survive.

But what makes this story so good is that her character reaches a dilemma. Finally, it becomes clear that she is definitely going to die. She is faced with a best bad choice situation: take her life into her own hands and end her own life OR keep fighting to survive even though she will suffer and almost certainly die anyway.

This dilemma is so important because it gives the character the chance to make a choice. Fighting for survival isn't a choice. Who wouldn't fight to survive? But when it becomes easier to *stop* fighting than it is to just *die*, then it leads to the dilemma.

Two Types of Story Dilemma

In *The Story Grid*, Shawn Coyne calls the dilemma the "crisis," and he distinguishes two types:

1. **Best Bad Choice.** The best bad choice dilemma is easy to understand. Just think of that game, "Would You Rather." You're given a choice between two horrible things. Which do you choose? For example, would you rather leave the love of your life at a party with another guy or let her humiliate you as she flirts with him? See? Drama, right? The inevitable consequence of a best bad choice will always be negative.
2. **Irreconcilable Goods.** Think of irreconcilable goods as the inverse of best bad choice decisions: both decisions will end positively for the character making the decision, but might cause a negative consequence for supporting characters. Another way to think about irreconcilable goods is that this decision pins two values that don't work together against one another. For example, love vs. money. Both are good, but like oil and water, they don't mix.

You can recognize these situations in your own life, right? We've all been through these dilemma moments, and the choices we make in the midst of them carry outsized consequences when compared to most of the little decisions we make in our lives.

Why Dilemmas Are the Foundation of Your Story

The dilemma is the central element of storytelling. It is the foundation of your story, the creator of drama, and the make-or-break moment in every story, act, and scene.

Without a dilemma, you have a series of events, not a story.

Why is the dilemma so important? The dilemma accomplishes two important functions:

1. Dilemmas Create Drama

All storytelling simulates the experiences of others for the reader.[1]

Studies of the brain show that when you read a phrase like, "As he walked down the steps, he slid his hand along the cool railing," it activates the same part of your brain as if you were actually experiencing it.

Novelist and psychologist Dr. Keith Oatley says that a story "runs on minds of readers just as computer simulations run on computers."

Amazingly, storytelling can create shared experiences for an audience, something all of us can experience together, even if none of us are actually *living* it.

But for the writer, just recreating experiences is not enough.

What hooks a reader, what drives them to read on, is *drama*, and the essence of drama is the following question: "If I were in this situation, how would I respond?"

In other words, drama is *choice*.

2. Dilemmas Characterize Your Protagonist

One characterization truism that is passed around writing circles is that for your protagonist to be a good character, he or she must make decisions.

We respond to characters who are *pro*active, not *re*active. No one wants to follow a hero or heroine who is simply letting life happen to them, never taking action, and never making decisions.

It's like an insipid new couple asking each other, "No, what do *you* want to eat for dinner? No, tell me what *you* want to eat for dinner. No, you. No, you!"

Gross.

We don't like these kinds of people in real life. We hate them in stories.

Someone must make a decision, and in a story, that person will usually be your protagonist.

Of course, knowing that your character must be proactive in theory is different than understanding how to apply it to your own writing process.

Have you ever been reading a book when you find yourself thinking, *There's no possible way this character can get out of this situation! This is just too bad. They're in way over their head, and there is no getting out of it.*

That is the moment of the dilemma. And readers love this moment. Why? Because we want to know what happens next!

A dilemma sets up a knowledge gap, and readers become desperate to fill that gap. It's in moments like this that readers are tempted to skip to the last page in the book just to find out if everything turns out okay (not that I've ever done that, of course).

The dilemma is what makes readers care about what happens—it's when we're encouraged to root for the main characters the most.

How I Added Dilemmas to My Memoir

For example, in my memoir, *Crowdsourcing Paris*, I realized it wasn't working because I didn't have any clear *dilemma*.

Things just *happened*.

I didn't set up clear literary crises, and therefore the choices my character was making didn't matter. Since the book is a memoir, I couldn't manufacture story crises, and so I had to pull them out of my actual experience.

One that I discovered in the first act of my story was a Best

Bad Choice story dilemma. In Paris, I wanted to live the "writer's life," where I hung out in cafés, drank coffee and wine, soaked up the atmosphere, people-watched, and wrote my book. But when my readers gave thousands of dollars to make me take on crowdsourced adventures, I had to choose between either refunding them money and being embarrassed or giving up my comfortable, "writerly" trip for an uncomfortable (but maybe more interesting) one.

I was able to take a dilemma that I was experiencing privately and turn it into a literary dilemma that centered my story.

Which just confirmed my awareness of how important a dilemma is in a story—and why we connect so vicariously to characters who need to make such decisions.

Dilemmas are all an important part of what creates movement in our day to day.

Dilemmas are what create defining moments.

Key Ideas

- The dilemma is the most important plot element. It is what the rising action builds toward and it forces a character to make a difficult decision.
- There are two types of dilemmas: **Best Bad Choice**, when both decisions will end negatively for the decider; and **Irreconcilable Goods**, the inverse of a Best Bad Choice, when two values that don't work together are pinned against each other.
- The dilemma is the central element of storytelling. It is what creates drama in a story, and without one, you have a series of events, not a story.
- Drama is choice and a dilemma is drama. People love drama. Drama is what hooks them.
- Dilemmas characterize your characters because

readers respond to characters who are proactive, not reactive.
- Dilemmas encourage readers to read forward because we care about what comes next—we need to know how the character makes this tough decision!

Practice

Story Analysis, Exercise One: Continue with the movie or book you chose for the last three exercises. First, pick one scene that you really like and find the dilemma in that scene. Then, spend fifteen minutes listing obstacles that build the action towards that choice. Starting immediately after the inciting incident, this is the scene's rising action.

Writing Practice, Exercise Two: What value is your story turning on, did you pick yet? If not, choose one of the main story values. Then, spend five minutes thinking of a scene that forces a choice between those values. Next, take ten minutes to come up with five possible complications based on that choice. It might also help to number them from one to five, with five being the obstacle that is the hardest.

Example: If I were writing *The Hunger Games* (moves on Life vs. Death), I might pick the scene where Katniss cuts down the tracker jacker nest. My list could then look like this:

Dilemma: Does Katniss cut the branch and potentially kill some of the tributes on the ground, or does she do nothing and die from starvation, dehydration, or the tributes waiting her out on the ground?

Then, I could list some interruptions that might upset her status quo like:

Rising Action/Progressive Complications:

1. Katniss sees the Tracker Jacker nest.

2. She tries to cut the branch holding it up but it's a thick branch.
3. Tracker Jackers start to sting Katniss.
4. The nest falls on the other tributes.
5. Katniss jumps out of the tree, while being continually stung, sees Glimmer dead with the bow and arrow in her hand.

11

ELEMENT 5: CLIMAX

This is the big moment!

This is the final showdown in a story (or scene) when we see a character *make* their crisis decision staged in the dilemma. Another way to put this is that the climax is the outcome of the dilemma, which you know now is the defining plot element in our list of six.

The fifth plot element on the list, the climax is the reason readers buy a book. It's the ultimate payoff to every plot event that has been set up throughout the story.

Everything is about to make sense.

Everything is about to be worth it—if you write your climax with the following writing tips.

As we move forward with a definition of climax and examples that will help you understand what makes an effective climax, keep in mind that a climax on the storywide scale is also when a protagonist achieves or loses their story's main desire.

A climax proves character transformation by unveiling how, in a final battle, a protagonist can defeat their antagonist because of what they've learned and who they've become.

The only reason a protagonist is ready is because they've

faced and overcome obstacles and dilemmas that have transformed them along the way.

This is also where we, as readers, witness the external plot and internal plot working in tandem. The protagonist makes their climatic decision because their previous dilemmas have prepared them to do what they need to do before the end.

Additionally, it's important to keep in mind that while a story's climax, which happens in the last third of the book, is why readers read your book, you need to include climaxes for every scene in your structure as well. The six elements of the plot are a package deal. They have separate purposes but work together.

The assimilation of them is what makes the story entertaining, insightful, and memorable.

Climax Definition

> The climax in a story is the point, usually near the end of the third act, where the character's choice in the dilemma plays out, leading to the moment of the greatest drama, action, and movement.

The Climax Is a Test of Value

Earlier we talked about how stories move, not through a heightened amount of conflict, although that's part of it, but through *values* in conflict.

If you put a traditional love story on a scale between love and hatred with ignorance in between and mapped out the values, then you might find that the story goes like this:

- **Exposition: Start in Ignorance.** The couple doesn't know each other, but then they meet and . . .
- **Inciting Incident: Loathing.** Things go . . . badly. He's a jerk and she hates him. The value goes down.

- **Rising Action:**
- **Part 1: Attraction.** In the midst of their hatred, something changes—he does something kind of noble—and all of that hatred turns into burning attraction.
- **Part 2 (Midpoint): Progressive Complications.** Something happens: maybe a rival from her past is introduced into mix, maybe he does something stupid, maybe she gets into danger in some extremely dangerous way, or maybe her family turns out to be crazy. Whatever happens, the couple separates, until . . .
- **Dilemma: Doubt.** It begins to look like they'll never get back together. Was it really meant to be? Maybe they're better off, maybe the *world* is better off, if they're apart.
- **Climax: Proof of love.** Nope. They *were* meant to be and one of them is going to prove it, either by driving across the country, or meeting the other in the airport, or interrupting their wedding to the rival, or saving them while sacrificing themselves, or some other dramatic way, all to show their love. The character acts on their decision to accomplish this choice.
- **Denouement: Reunited.** The wedding, the ride off into the sunset, the happy ending, all is well, the end. (We'll cover the meaning of this final plot element next.)

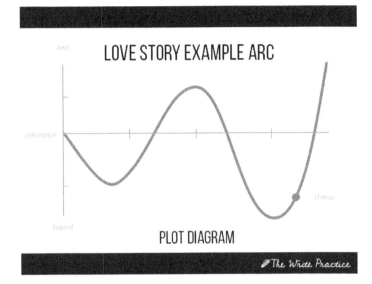

Stories that follow this structure include *Pride and Prejudice*, *Twilight*, *Pearl Harbor*, and more.

For our purposes, though, take special note of the climax, in this case the Proof of Love scene. In a thriller, this wouldn't be a proof of love scene, it would be called a "hero at the mercy of a villain" scene. Or if it were a mystery, it would be the "detective explains how the murder happened" scene, perhaps putting himself/herself into the crosshairs of the villain. Or if it were an adventure story, it would be the big, final, life vs. death battle.

The point is, the climax *changes* based on the value of the story.

In other words, the climax is the moment where the core value of a story is put to the final test.

Some people say you need more action in a climax, but you only need action in an action story. All climaxes are about *values* in conflict, not conflict for its own sake. So figure out what value your story is about, then tap into it and create conflict that impacts the value shift.

How the Climax Fits into the Dramatic Structure

The climax is the fifth and penultimate element in the dramatic structure, occurring just after the dilemma and just before the denouement or resolution.

Since the denouement is usually just one or two scenes long, the climax is usually very close to the end of a story, often the second-to-last or third-to-last scene (although sometimes longer denouements are required, leaving the climax further from the end).

Some stories also have the story's chief climax at the end of the second act, not the third. In these cases, there may still be a smaller climax near the end of the story, but it will be reduced in movement and intensity.

How Long Is the Climax in a Story?

The climax usually is just one scene, and while it doesn't take up much space in the story, especially compared to the rising action, it is often the longest scene in the book because so much has to happen. For example, the final battle in an adventure story may only be one scene but take 5,000 words to tell.

How Freytag's Pyramid Gets Climax Wrong

Freytag's climax is different from the understanding we hold today in two main areas: where he puts the climax and what the climax is.

Let's start with *where* Freytag considers the climax to be.

Where the Climax is in Freytag's Pyramid

For Freytag, the climax was in the center of a story, not toward the end. See the plot diagram found in *Freytag's Technique of the Drama* below:

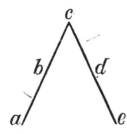

These parts of the drama, (*a*) introduction, (*b*) rise, (*c*) climax, (*d*) return or fall, (*e*) catastrophe, have each what is peculiar in purpose and in construction.

The top of the triangle, marked "C," is the climax, according to Freytag. However, most writers today would put the climax much later in the story. See the comparison of Freytag's Pyramid to other story structures:

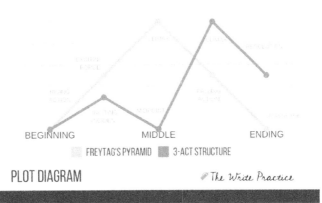

Notice how the climax comes much later in the story.

While writers today would consider the climax of most stories near the end of the plot, for Freytag, it's in the center.

But that's not the only difference.

What the Climax is in Freytag's Pyramid

The second difference is how Freytag *defines* the climax.

Freytag's "climax" is much different from how we would think of the climax today. As we talked about, Freytag was particularly interested in a single story arc, what we call the "Icarus" arc.

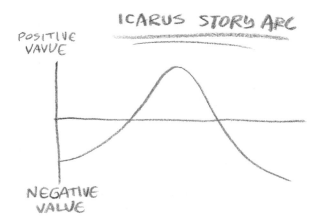

For Freytag, the climax of the story was the peak of the pyramid, the moment when the character's fortunes reverse.

In *Romeo and Juliet*, according to Freytag, this was the moment when Romeo says goodbye to Juliet, now his wife, immediately after killing Tybalt and being exiled.

Today, no one would call that the climax of *Romeo and Juliet*. Instead, most writers would consider that the midpoint, calling the scene in which the lovers commit suicide the climax.

Freytag is still the source of much confusion because of this misunderstanding. Many writing teachers share Freytag's Pyramid without understanding he was working with a very different climax than we would use today.

Thus, be cautious about anyone who teaches Freytag's Pyramid and places the climax in or near the center of the story, because it's unlikely they know the origin of Freytag's ideas and his different understanding of climax.

Climax Examples

To get a better understanding of how climaxes work in stories, let's look at a few examples from a variety of stories.

Harry Potter and the Sorcerer's Stone

How does the climax in the first novel in the Harry Potter series work? Spoiler alert!

The climax: Harry Potter and Professor Quirrell/Voldemort's shadow-self have a major showdown in the forbidden third-floor corridor, ending with Harry saving the Philosopher's Stone from Voldemort, which hinders Voldemort's plans to return to power.

In the climax, Harry realizes that Voldemort, who we previously thought was dead, in fact survived the spell that rebounded on him and has been gathering strength through Quirrell's help.

When the climax occurs: The third-to-last scene.

The value the climax is testing: Life vs. death. As an adventure story, *Harry Potter and the Sorcerer's Stone* moves between the value of life and its negation, death. In the climax, it is this value that is tested, as Harry is overmatched by both Professor Quirrell and Voldemort's shadow and very nearly dies.

There is also a secondary, internal value: education vs. naïveté, as Harry has to apply everything he's learned at Hogwarts to survive.

Outcome of the climax: Harry faints, surviving the encounter only because Professor Dumbledore arrives just in time, proving both that Harry is courageous and also that he is not yet a match for Voldemort.

Subplot climax: *Harry Potter and the Sorcerer's Stone* has a performance subplot with the value scale of accomplishment vs. failure. The scenes that follow the climax, which are part of the denouement, are actually the climaxes of the subplot, ending with the victory of winning the Hogwarts House Cup.

Ready Player One

How does the climax in the novel *Ready Player One* work (the novel version, of course!)? Spoiler alert!

The climax: The climax of *Ready Player One* has two parts.

The first part is the battle between the Gunters and the Sixers over control of the final gate. The battle ends when the Sixers detonate the Cataclyst, wiping out every player in the sector *except* for Wade Watts, the protagonist, who had an extra life token, and is then able to enter the final gate.

The second part of the climax is when Wade goes through Halliday's final test: finding the correct system to play *Tempest* on, beating *Tempest*, and speaking the memorized lines from *Monty Python and the Holy Grail*.

When the climax occurs: The third and fourth final scenes.

The value the climax is testing: Life vs. death. As an adventure story, *Ready Player One* lands on the life and death scale. It includes "digital death" *and* a sense of real-life death, as the Sixers have the ability to do both (putting real-life death on the table is an important aspect of plots involving alternate worlds like *Ready Player One*, *The Matrix*, and *Tron*).

There is also an internal value of good vs. evil at stake in the climax, evil being personified in the Sixers but also present, to some degree, in Halliday's isolation and self-centered obsession with the OASIS, something he later regrets and attempts to weed out of his successor.

Outcome of the climax: Wade retrieves Halliday's egg from the game *Adventure*, completing the quest, and winning control of the OASIS.

Subplot climax: *Ready Player One* has a love story subplot which finds its climax in the final scene of the story as Wade and Samantha meet and then kiss for the first time in the real world.

4 Tips to Write a Great Climax

How do you write an amazing climax? Here are a few tips:

1. Focus on Your Story's Values, Not Just More "Conflict" or "Action"

Many people think that the climax is the moment of highest conflict or the most amount of action, and for some stories, that's certainly appropriate. However, the main purpose of the climax is to bring about the biggest reversal of fortunes of your character.

Too often, we mistake our character's fortunes with the arc of the story, and while fortune is involved, it's not the main criterion of our story arc.

Instead, see how the purpose of the climax is to have the most conflict *between the values* in your story, and the greatest amount of *movement* in those values, especially since this is the moment readers have been waiting for since they started reading the book. This means that the greatest change in your characters' fortunes happens *because* of those values, and how they shift determines if your protagonist is victorious or not—i.e., if they achieve the goal established very early in the story, when they decided to take on their adventure at the end of act one.

So before you write your story's climax, find the values

driving your story's main plot. It will be one of the six values we discussed earlier in this book:

1. Life vs. Death
2. Life vs. a Fate *Worse* than Death
3. Love vs. Hate
4. Accomplishment vs. Failure
5. Maturity vs. Naïveté
6. Good vs. Evil

Set those values in the exposition. Begin their movement in the exposition. Raise and lower them through the rising action. And finally, put them to the final test in the climax.

2. Most Stories Have Two or Three Plots, Which Means They Need Two or Three Climaxes

There is always one core plot, one core value, and one core climax. However, most stories have multiple plotlines, almost always two and sometimes three, including:

- The main plot
- The internal plot
- The subplot

We talked elsewhere about subplots, but what is an internal and external plot? It all comes down to the values in action in the story.

As we talked about above, there are six values in storytelling. Internal plots focus on the final two value scales:

- Maturity vs. Naïveté
- Good vs. Evil

External plots, on the other hand, focus on the first four value scales:

- Life vs. Death
- Life vs. a Fate *Worse* than Death
- Love vs. Hate
- Accomplishment vs. Failure

Most commercially successful stories have an external plot, and many—although not all—also have an internal plot.

When combined with the subplot, that leaves three plotlines, and each of these storylines or plotlines need their own climax.

How do you write *three* climaxes, though?

Often, the external and internal climaxes combine, as we see above in the examples from *Ready Player One* and *Harry Potter and the Sorcerer's Stone*, in the form of one major climax or a two-part climax. More on this in the next tip.

Another habit of great storytellers, whether conscious or unconscious, is to put the climax of the subplot in the last scene of the denouement, effectively bringing the story to completion.

By the way, one of the major flaws of the film version of *Ready Player One* was that they had already resolved the love story subplot, and so there was little tension left in the final scene, leaving the plot to end with a whimper.

3. The Internal Climax Makes Possible the External Climax

Not all stories have an internal plot, but if yours does, a good way to set up the external climax is often through the internal climax.

For example, it is Wade Watts's decision in *Ready Player One* to share the prize with his friends if he wins Halliday's contest that propels him into the final test and shows that he has what it takes to learn Halliday's lesson.

In the same way, everything Harry learned at Hogwarts is necessary for the final showdown with Quirrell/Voldemort.

The internal plot, if there is one, sets up the external plot.

4. If Your Climax Isn't Working, Look to the Dilemma

The dilemma is the center of your story, the most important of all six elements. It is also the thing that *most* pushes your story into the climax.

What that means is if you're writing or editing your climax and you feel like it's not working, go back to the dilemma and start there to figure things out.

Why is the dilemma so important to the success of the climax?

The dilemma is always the presentation of a difficult choice, either between two bad things or two good things. It is *here* that the values in your story begin to be tested.

The dilemma *isn't* where the protagonist *makes* that choice. It is where the choice is presented.

The climax, on the other hand, is where the protagonist makes the choice, and the urgency and agency of that decision is what drives the consequences, and thus the action, of the climax.

But if you don't have a dilemma, or if the choice your protagonist is facing doesn't have significantly high enough stakes, then the dilemma won't work.

And thus, the climax will fall short.

Climaxes for Subplots and Scenes

One final thing to note is that stories have more than one climax. In fact, every act and *scene* should have its own climax.

Of course, there will be one **core climax** in the main plotline. This is the big moment that turns on the main plot's value shift, and it leads up to the final showdown that readers have been waiting to read. However, there are smaller climaxes in each scene and act, all of which continue to create drama and keep the story moving along its value scale.

Subplots contain their own climax as well, and the subplot climax has a uniquely important role in most stories.

That's because the best place for the subplot climax is the denouement, the final scene or scenes in a story, which is what we'll talk about in the next section.

That's why all too often, a story with a love story subplot will end with a final kiss between the protagonist and their love interest, bringing the subplot to completion.

It's important to pay attention to both the core climax and also the climax for your subplot.

Key Ideas

- The climax is the point, usually near the end of the third act, where the value of the story is tested to its highest degree. As such, it is also the moment in a story with the greatest amount of drama, action, and movement.
- The climax *changes* based on the value of the story. In other words, the climax is the moment where the core value of a story is put to the final test.
- More action isn't what makes a climax great (although you do need more action in an action/adventure story). Climaxes are about *values* in conflict, not conflict for its own sake.
- The climax is usually very close to the end of a story, often the second-to-last or third-to-last scene.
- The climax usually is just one scene, and while it doesn't take up much space in the story, especially

compared to the rising action, it is often the longest scene in the book.
- There are multiple climaxes in a story. The main climax moves on the story's core value, but one of the most important climaxes besides the story's core climax is the climax in the subplot.
- The best place for the subplot climax is the denouement, the final scene or scenes in a story.
- Freytag is the source of much confusion when it comes to climaxes because Freytag puts the climax of the story at the peak of Freytag's Pyramid, the moment when the character's fortunes reverse. Many writing teachers share Freytag's Pyramid without understanding he was working with a very different climax than we would use today. So the definition and where a climax really happens is different today than when Freytag created Freytag's Pyramid.

Practice

Story Analysis Exercise: Continue with the movie or book you chose for the last four exercises. Look for the climax in the last third of the movie or book. I bet this will be pretty obvious.

Next, spend fifteen minutes looking at how exposition, an inciting incident, rising action, and a dilemma all work in the climax. Last, spend fifteen minutes journaling about how the protagonist *acts* on their choice in the climax.

P.S. Make sure to include how they've succeeded or failed to 1) transform (they're a different character than they were in the beginning of the story), 2) get or lose their story goal/want/desire, and 3) defeat or fall to their main antagonist.

Writing Practice Exercise: Spend fifteen minutes outlining your story's climax by choosing the dilemma in your climax and then jotting down how the other plot elements build to it.

Once you know your story's dilemma in the climax scene, write a few sentences about how your protagonist acts on their crisis decision.

Example: If I were writing the climax for *The Hunger Games* (moves on Life vs. Death), I might journal this:

Dilemma: Kill Peeta or don't after the rules are revoked again?

Climax: After the rules are revoked again, announcing that only one tribute can survive the games, Katniss looks at Peeta, and Peeta tells her to kill him. Katniss has fallen for Peeta, if not in love than as a friend, so she can't do this. However, Katniss realizes something about the Capitol: they need a victor! So Katniss proposes to Peeta that they eat nightlark together and choose death as one instead of against one another. They take the risk and count down from three, but right before eating the berries, they're both announced victors!

12

ELEMENT 6: DENOUEMENT

We've reached the end of the story, also known as the denouement, which determines how your story actually ends. Tragedy or triumph. Wedding or funeral. Alive or dead.

In the final essential plot element, a story establishes "normal" all over again—but the new normal, incorporating the changes and experiences of your characters.

For fans of the Hero's Journey, this is where, in a story's whole, the protagonist returns home with the reward.

Your readers get to sit with your characters a little in their new normal. You emotionally wrap everything up so your reader can put the book away without flipping back through the pages to see what they missed. It's a scene closure with enough finality to deserve those two words: The End.

We put the book down and allow ourselves to be swept away with lasting thoughts and emotions.

Denouement Definition

Denouement (pronounced day-new-mah) is a literary term referring to the final part of a narrative, usually in which the outcome of the story is revealed and the character and audience have a moment to dwell on the events of the story.

The Denouement Resolves the Story

Denouement came from the French language (thus, the extra "e"!) in the 18th century and means, literally, "untying." In the case of a story, it means "the untying of the plot."

The idea is that the tension in a story builds through to the climax, and in the denouement, also known as the resolution, that tension is untied.

In dramatic structure, denouement is the final part, the moment when all the pieces must be put in their place, and when the author will leave us with our final image of the story.

After the climax, most stories wrap up quite quickly, within one or two scenes.

That means that the denouement, as the final part of a story, is generally one or two scenes long.

Examples of Denouement

The denouement is a relatively short part of a story, but it's also one of the most important pieces, since this is the ending the audience has been waiting for throughout the story. Often, this is the part readers *most* remember from the story, the part which lingers in their minds long after they finish reading or watching.

Here are a few examples of denouements from literature:

Romeo and Juliet

In the climax of the story, Romeo mistakenly thinks Juliet has died and decides to drink poison to end his own life. As he's dying, Juliet wakes up, and when he finally dies, she decides to take her own life as well.

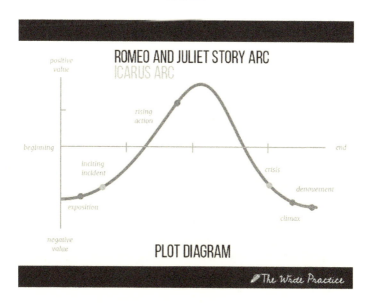

The denouement begins just after the couple's death, starting from their discovery by their families and Friar Laurence. Only one scene long, it begins with a monologue from Friar Laurence, includes a reconciliation between the two families, and ends with a final monologue from the Prince.

Length: one scene

Ready Player One

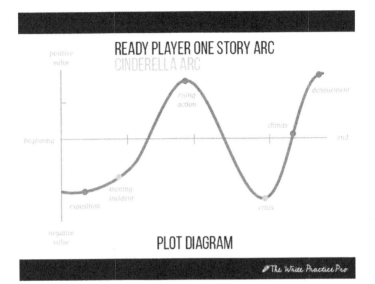

The denouement occurs after the big fight with the evil, corporate Sixers, and after Wade Watts collects the final prize from Halliday.

The denouement consists of two short scenes, both of which take place once he's back in the real world.

The first scene of the denouement is a brief interaction with Ogden Morrow, cofounder of the OASIS alongside Halliday, in which he cements the lessons from the story, alludes to Watts's fortune, and reveals the Sixers' leader's arrest.

The final scene of the denouement and the novel as a whole takes place at the first real-life meeting between Watts and his love interest, Art3mis, Samantha in real life.

Length: two scenes

The Hobbit

The dragon, terrifying as he is, is just a preamble for a

larger battle between the armies of humans, elves, and dwarves against an army of goblins. Finally, the hobbit gets his treasure and returns back to the Shire.

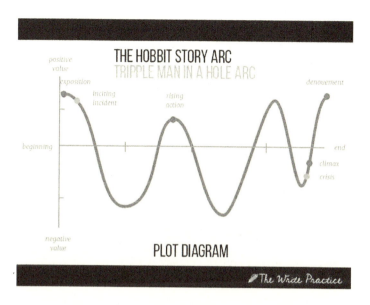

The Hobbit is a complicated plot with a triple (or even quadruple) Man in a Hole structure, and as such, the denouement is a bit longer and more elaborate, and in the end, more of a montage of the journey home than a set of specific scenes.

For *The Hobbit* the denouement includes:

- The characters hold funerals and mourn the fallen from the battle
- Bilbo and the dwarves receive their treasure (which Bilbo gives up)
- Bilbo says goodbye to the dwarves and is praised by the elves
- A journey to Beorn's, where Bilbo recuperates
- Travelling back to Rivendell, home of the elves
- A lot of elven songs (I'm not a fan of all the songs!)

- Travelling back to the the Shire and to Bilbo's hobbit hole with Gandalf
- Bilbo discovers everyone thought he was dead and his relatives had moved into his house
- Bilbo puts everything to right and is once again comfortable, but he does often visit the elves
- Several years later, Gandalf and one of the dwarves visits Bilbo again and they reminisce

There's a great quote from Gandalf near the end of the denouement that illustrates both Bilbo's evolution as a character and also the purpose of the denouement:

"My dear Bilbo!" [Gandalf] said, "Something is the matter with you! You are not the hobbit that you were."

How to Write the Denouement: Three Tips

If you're writing a novel, screenplay, or other narrative, how do you write a great denouement? Here are three tips:

1. Make Sure One Exists

You'd be surprised at how many writers choose to end their stories at the end of the climax and forego the denouement, thinking it's better to end on a high note.

It never works.

The reader needs one or two scenes to come down off the action, look around, and see how the world has changed now, past the action of the story.

2. Show the New World Order

The purpose of the denouement is to give the reader a chance to see the new world order.

The exposition and denouement are in many ways mirrors of each other.

If you're stuck on what to write in your denouement, focus on how the world looks now compared to how the world looked in the exposition.

3. End With the Subplot

One of the best uses for the denouement is to cap off the subplot, if you have one. This is especially effective if you have a love story subplot.

For example, in *Ready Player One*, the final scene of the denouement completes the love story arc between Wade Watts and Art3mis.

This is a great way to finish your subplot efficiently while also ending your main plot effectively. Try it out!

How Will YOU End Your Story?

All stories must end. But *how* you end it can make or break your story.

Understanding what the denouement in a story is, plus using the tips above, will make your story all the better.

Key Ideas

- Denouement (pronounced day-new-mah) is a literary term referring to the final part of a narrative, usually in which the outcome of the story is revealed. Here, the tension built through to the climax is untied.
- The denouement, as the final part of a story, is generally one or two scenes long.
- Readers often remember the denouement *most* because it's the ending they've been waiting to see.
- Use three tips to write the denouement: make sure

one exists, show the new world order, and end with a subplot.

Practice

Story Analysis Exercise: Continue with the movie or book you chose for the exposition practice exercise. Now, look at the last scene of the story. Is it a subplot? How does it show the new world order? What's the last lingering emotion? Journal about this for fifteen minutes.

Writing Practice Exercise: Look back at your story's core climax and any subplots you've created in your structure. For five minutes, using the six plot elements, write out your denouement's structure for your core story. Make sure to use the three tips for writing the denouement to do this.

Example: If I were writing *The Hunger Games*, I might journal this:

Denouement: Katniss and Peeta return home on a train as victors. This shows how Katniss is returning to a new world order (she's a victor but also President Snow's number one enemy) and ends with a subplot (internal plot of coming-of-age and also clarification of the love illusion staged in the games).

1. Exposition: Katniss and Peeta bored the train.
2. Inciting Incident: Peeta asks what happens when they get back.
3. Rising Action: Katniss wants to pretend like nothing happened but Peeta doesn't want to forget. Katniss returns to her family and Gale.
4. Dilemma: Katniss can pretend she's in love with Peeta to protect her family or not.
5. Climax: Katniss and Peeta put on a happy face for the crowds.
6. Denouement: Katniss knows that even as a victor, she will never escape the Capitol.

Not Included: Falling Action

One term you won't see in The Write Structure framework is falling action, which is usually defined as the part meant to wind the story down from the climax to the resolution and the story's end.

We don't use this term for a number of reasons, including the fact that it's confusing and largely useless. If you'd like a full explanation of how the falling action is supposed to work in story structure and why we omit it from our framework, you can find it in Appendix B.

PART IV

MAKING STRUCTURE WORK FOR YOUR WRITING

How do you take the ideas and theories that we've learned and actually put them to use to write your novel, screenplay, memoir, or short story?

In the following chapters, I'm going to show you exactly how I write my books, from what to do *before* you outline your book and the way through the plotting process and the writing of the first draft.

If you're ready to stop *learning* and get *writing*, the practical steps and tips you'll learn in this section are for you.

13

WHAT TO DO BEFORE YOU START STRUCTURING

In the previous chapters, we've covered the building blocks of story, and how plot and structure not only navigate drama on an important timeline, but also how a story's arc and value shifts determine essential elements that advance a plot with purpose.

This is fantastic.

You need to know and understand everything we've covered about plot and structure in order to write a great book. But that understanding will fall short when you actually *write* that book if you don't understand how to *apply* those elements into your pre-writing process.

You need a practical plan before you structure your novel.

You need crucial steps that will make your writing process more manageable and purposeful because you know why you're writing *this* story, and just as importantly, why it's important to meet your deadlines along the way.

Still, setting deadlines will do nothing but discourage you if you struggle to actually meet them with raging success.

To help you complete your steps, you need more than benchmarks.

You need to set consequences to make you accountable—

motivators that prevent you from falling into the trap of overplanning and procrastination.

Using a system like the one I used to finish my best-selling book can keep you focused and enthusiastic throughout the whole writing process, from basic bare bones to edited final draft.

Before You Structure

The point of all of this is not to give you another excuse to not write your book. Also, the point is not to come up with the perfect structure and outline. Perfectionism at any point in the writing process is destructive, but perfectionism is especially harmful during the prewriting and planning phase. There's no better way to procrastinate than to spend time "planning" your book.

Why is overplanning so dangerous?

Because your writing will *never* live up to your preconception. No matter how good of a writer you are, how you imagine your book will be before you start writing will outpace your actual writing.

Instead, make a plan but don't overplan. Set deadlines and create consequences.

First, Set Deadlines

Before you do anything else, you need to set a deadline for when you're going to finish the first draft of your novel.

Stephen King said a first draft should be written in no more than a season, so ninety days.

In our 100 Day Book Program, we give people a little longer than that, a hundred days, which seems like a good length of time for most people.

I recommend setting your deadline for no longer than four months. If it's longer than that, you'll procrastinate. A good length of time to write a book is something that makes you a little nervous, but not outright terrified.

Then, mark the deadline date in your calendar, kneel on the floor, close your eyes, and make a vow to yourself and your book idea that you will write the first draft of your novel by then, no matter what.

A final deadline alone isn't enough, though. You also have to set smaller deadlines.

A novel can't be written in a day. There's no way to "cram" for a novel. The key to writing a novel is to make a little progress every day.

If you write a thousand words a day, something most people are capable of doing in an hour or two, for a hundred days, by the end you'll have a 100,000 word novel, which is a pretty long novel!

So set smaller, weekly deadlines that break up your book into pieces. I recommend trying to write 5,000 to 6,000 words per week by each Friday or Sunday, whichever works best for you.

If you can hit all of your weekly deadlines, you know you'll make your final deadline at the end.

But Deadlines Alone Aren't Enough. You Need to Create Consequences.

You might be thinking, *Setting a deadline is fine, but how do I actually hit my deadline?* Here's the secret I learned from my friend Tim Grahl.

Create a consequence. Here's how:

1. Set your deadline.
2. Write a check to an organization or nonprofit you hate. (When I did this, it was during the 2016 U.S. presidential election, and I wrote a check to the

campaign of the candidate I liked least, who shall remain nameless!)
3. Then think of two other, minor consequences (like giving up your favorite TV show for a month or having to buy ice cream for everyone at work).
4. Give your check, plus your list of two minor consequences, to a friend you trust with firm instructions to hold you to your consequences if you don't meet your deadlines.
5. If you miss one of your weekly deadlines, you get one of your minor consequences (e.g. giving up your favorite TV show).
6. If you miss THREE weekly deadlines OR if you miss the final deadline, your check gets sent to the organization you hate.
7. Finally, write! I promise you, if you do steps 1–6, you will be incredibly focused!

When I did this while writing my seventh book, I finished it in just sixty-three days. It was the most focused I've ever been in my life!

Before I started using consequences, I struggled to finish books, getting bogged down in research, perfectionism, and yes, structure. But since I began creating consequences (or having consequences created for me), I've finished more than a dozen books.

Consequences work, so before you start structuring, set a deadline and create a consequence!

Key Ideas

- Plan, but don't overplan. You don't want to use planning as an excuse to procrastinate actually writing your book.
- Set a small timeline to complete your first draft. I

recommended a hundred days, and have seen success with this window with my own work and with Write Practice's 100 Day Book program.
- You (probably) won't meet your deadlines if there aren't consequences. Set negative consequences for not meeting your benchmarks, and get someone you trust to hold you accountable.

Practice

Exercise: Set a deadline and create a consequence. To make this easier, I created The Write Plan planner to guide writers through the novel planning process. You can download a free worksheet from this planner at thewritepractice.com/structure.

14

MAKE YOUR NOVEL IDEA BETTER

Out of the thousands of aspiring authors I've talked to over the years, most think the most important step to writing a best-selling, award winning book is to have a great idea.

Occasionally, these writers come up with an idea so exciting, so powerful, that they can't help but just start writing. Maybe they do a quick outline first, possibly after hearing that this is something you should do beforehand. *Then* they start writing.

They write for a day or a week or a month or even longer, but then something happens.

Huh, this isn't as good as what I imagined in my head, they think when they go back and read some of what they've written. *This doesn't feel like my original idea.*

Then they go back and revise. Or they return to their outline in an effort to make it better. But this is just the beginning of a spiral that after a day or a month or a year leaves them burnt out with the writing process, their book abandoned, and them hating their idea and, sometimes, their own lack of talent and discipline.

This is actually how I used to approach writing, too. And it's one of the reasons I spent more than a decade trying to write a novel and failing.

But the promise of The Write Structure is that all of this can be avoided, and the first step to avoid it is to give up the idea that the most important step to writing a book is to have an idea.

"Ideas are cheap," said George R.R. Martin. "Execution is all that matters."

Before I became a published author, I had these very elaborate, extreme ideas, these ideas that I thought were going to make me like the great American novelist, you know?

And they had six different plots and so much was going on in those stories. They were going to be amazing.

But what I realized as I became a published author is that the best ideas are really simple.

Simple ideas are clear.

Simple ideas are achievable.

Simple ideas put the focus on your *writing*.

Write a simple idea, not because it's the best book idea in the history of writing, but because this isn't going to be your last book, and the most important thing you can do as a writer is to *finish* your *next* book.

How do you make sure your idea is simple enough that you can actually finish it?

Craft your idea into a single sentence premise.

What Is a Premise?

A premise takes your whole book idea and distills it down to a single sentence with three essential components.

Is it really possible to summarize an entire book idea in just a single sentence? Yes! And all it takes is three simple elements.

If you're writing fiction, it contains the following three pieces:

1. A protagonist
2. A goal
3. A situation, crisis, or antagonist

In this chapter we'll talk about each of these, but first, the magic of a premise is that when you can get your book idea down to a single sentence you can do amazing things with it:

- You have a ready-made pitch for your novel that you can give to agents and publishers or use to prove to your friends and family that you're serious!
- When you get lost during the writing process, you have a guide to get yourself back on track.
- And you actually have the first and most important part of a book proposal.
- Best of all, just through that single sentence, you can take your okay idea and help turn it into a best-selling idea.

And yes, it *is* important to pare your idea down to a single sentence. In fact, some agents' proposal formats actually require a single sentence description, so that's something to be really disciplined about. Remember your premise doesn't have to contain everything in your story. Just these three most essential bits.

I have spent months working on this ONE sentence, writing and rewriting it to make it work. In one book, I wrote hundreds of different versions of the premise before I finally settled on the one premise that worked. Not long after that, my book was picked up by a literary agent.

If your premise isn't working, then you know your book isn't working, and so you can often spot problems in your book with this simple sentence.

Premise Examples

To show you how a premise works, here are a few examples:

> A <u>young girl</u> is *swept away to a magical land in a tornado and embarks on a quest to see the wizard* who can help her **return home.** —*The Wizard of Oz* by L. Frank Baum

Here's another, the premise of my novel:

> A <u>normal teen</u> becomes a virtuoso violinist and **enters to win the top violin competition in the world** when *his best friend, a prodigy, is killed in a car accident and he inherits his possessed violin.*

See the three pieces in action?
<u>Underlined</u> = protagonist
Bold = goal
Italics = situation/crisis/antagonist

I've helped hundreds of authors improve their book ideas, and this tool that we've been talking about, a single-sentence premise, is the best tool I've found to make your idea better. You can fix so many future problems in your novel just by working on your premise.

So let's put it to practice with your book idea.

Premise Step One: A Protagonist

Let's go deeper by talking about each piece of the premise, starting with the protagonist.

Protagonist Definition

A protagonist is the central character in a story, sometimes called the hero or main character.

The protagonist, according to Stephen Koch's *The Modern Library Writer's Workshop*, is the character whose fate matters most to the story.

The Protagonist in Your Premise

In your single sentence premise, your task is to capture your protagonist as briefly and fully as possible, traditionally in two words: one adjective and one noun.

The adjective should give us a brief insight into their character. For example, a "naive teen" or a "jaded detective" or a "lonely orphan" or a "talented basketball player."

The noun should not be the protagonist's name. Instead, it should further describe the character. For example, if you were to write a premise for The Wizard of Oz, you wouldn't say "kind-hearted Dorothy," but "a kind-hearted girl," which gives a little information on the character's age and gender.

Try to be as specific as possible. You only have two words, so make them count.

What if You Have More Than One Protagonist?

Maybe you have multiple central characters in your story, even a *team* of heroes and heroines, and you're wondering if you can make them *all* protagonists.

In stories with multiple central characters, it is important to distinguish between protagonists and point-of-view characters.

Point-of-view characters are characters whose point of view the narrative takes when in first- or third-person limited perspective.

In some novels with multiple points of view, the chapter begins with the name of the character.

Having multiple points of view is considered an advanced skill in storytelling because it's so difficult to pull off well and so easy to mess up. Even George R.R. Martin, a master storyteller when he began writing *Game of Thrones*, struggled with the many different perspectives in his *Song of Ice and Fire* series.

One thing to note about point-of-view characters is that they are not always the protagonist. For example, F. Scott Fitzgerald's *The Great Gatsby* is told from the point of view of Nick Carraway, but the protagonist is Jay Gatsby.

Also, while you can have many point-of-view characters, it doesn't mean you have multiple protagonists. Just because you take a character's POV doesn't mean they are a protagonist.

Now that we're clear on the difference between protagonists and point-of-view characters, what if you *still* believe you have multiple protagonists by necessity? Unless you're writing a saga, meaning a multi-POV story spanning multiple books, you *should* only have one protagonist. And even if you *are* writing an eight-book saga with eleven POV characters, you probably still have one protagonist.

"What about Game of Thrones?" you might ask. "Doesn't it have multiple protagonists?"

First, if you've been successfully writing and publishing novels and writing screenplays that get filmed for thirty years like George R.R. Martin, then I think you can do whatever you want, whatever the "rules" say. Assuming you haven't, I would suggest starting with something a bit easier.

On a more esoteric note, when I think about George RR Martin's song of *Ice and Fire* and other stories that follow many different characters, I would find it very challenging to write a premise.

So in that situation, there are two practical solutions:

1. The world can become the protagonist (Westeros for Martin).
2. You can choose the character you think the story really revolves around the most. For example, in *Game of Thrones*, you might argue the television series revolves around Tyrion or Bran or Jon Snow,

so you might focus on one of their plotlines in the premise.

Or perhaps you're writing a love story about a couple falling for each other. In that case, choose one of the characters you most want to follow, asking the question, "Whose fate drives this story?"

For example, in *Pride and Prejudice*, it's Elizabeth and Mr. Darcy's story, but it's really Elizabeth's fate that drives the story.

Why is it so important to choose one character? One of the reasons you have to pick one is that you have to figure out what their goal is.

So let's look at the protagonist's goal next.

Premise Step Two: A Goal

There are three criteria to consider when you're developing your protagonist's goal.

The protagonist must have a worthwhile goal, one that shows they are taking agency in their own lives. This goal should be based as far into the action of the story as possible, preferably near the climax or resolution. The goal should also point to the value scale and plot type you're writing.

Let's look at each of these statements and how they work in your premise.

Is your protagonist passive or active?

The biggest mistake writers make in their premise is the "passive protagonist."

As readers, we DON'T want to read about someone who is just along for the ride, who never makes decisions. As we've talked about, good structure *requires* characters to make decisions. In the same way, your premise needs to highlight a character's agency.

The goal element of a good premise needs to show that

your protagonist is taking their fate in their hands, right or wrong, win or lose.

If you look closely at your favorite characters, you'll see that they are constantly making decisions.

Harry Potter chooses to be in Gryffindor even when he could have gone into Slytherin.

Luke Skywalker chooses to help Princess Leia with Old Ben even when he could have stayed in Tatooine.

Holden Caulfield chooses to leave his prep school and goes to New York.

Look at your own premise. Is your protagonist taking action? Are they *avoiding* taking action?

Because no one wants to read a story about a character whom a lot of things happen to but who never makes any choices. Don't fall into the "passive protagonist" trap, and start right here in your premise.

Where does your character's goal take place in the story?

Think about your story as a whole. Ideally, the goal that you share in your premise is at the climax.

Remember, the purpose of the premise is a tool *for you*, not to share with readers. Don't worry about spoiling the ending. Instead, use the goal to point to the ending, the climactic moment at the end of your story. You don't necessarily have to give *away* the ending, but it should let us know where the story is going.

For example, in the example above from *The Wizard of Oz*, Dorothy's goal to return home doesn't happen until the last scene of the story.

This is important because this will help you figure out the value scale and plot type of the story you're trying to tell.

Is your value scale and plot type present in the premise?

Can you easily tell what type of story you're trying to tell from your premise? See the plot types and scales below if you've forgotten.

Plot Types

1. **Life vs. Death:** Action, Adventure
2. **Life vs. a Fate *Worse* than Death:** Thriller, Horror, Mystery/Crime
3. **Love vs. Hate:** Love Story, Romance
4. **Accomplishment vs. Failure:** Performance, Sports
5. **Maturity vs. Naïveté:** Coming-of-Age
6. **Good vs. Evil:** Temptation, Morality

Are you telling an action story? Could you be telling a love story?

This is one reason it's helpful to make the goal as far into the story as possible, because it allows you to get clues for your type and scale.

By the way, any agent or prospective reader is *also* looking for clues as to the type of story you're telling, and by including them here, you give yourself a chance to hook them.

This premise will help you at every stage of your writing process, so be really clear about what your character's goal is. Make the goal as far into the action of the story as possible. And make sure the character isn't passive, but actively taking their fate into their hands, making choices, and overcoming obstacles for the sake of their goals.

BUT even the best goal doesn't work without a situation or crisis that pushes the protagonist to their limits, so let's talk about that next.

Premise Step Three: A Situation

We've already talked about two elements of a single-sentence novel premise: the goal and the protagonist. Now, let's focus on the third and final element, the situation.

This is usually the hardest part of writing a premise

because how do you take a whole book, a huge story, and capture it all in a single sentence?

And the answer, of course, is that you don't! You can't! But what you can do is get the single most important bit.

If you can figure out what the most important part of your premise is, then you instantly have made a compass, a tool that will guide you in your writing process whenever you get lost. This single sentence can save your novel writing process.

So how do you determine what situation or crisis to focus on?

First, when you're thinking about the situation, it's helpful to consider two things: the inciting incident, the event that kicks off the action of the story; and also the climax, where the character is finally confronting that antagonist or that big problem.

Another way to get to the heart of your situation is to introduce the antagonist. If you don't have an antagonist, that's okay too. Just try to focus on the biggest problem the character is facing in the story.

Antagonist Definition

An antagonist is a character who works *against* the goals of the protagonist and who is often immoral or evil.

An antagonist is a classic archetype seen in almost every story from Shakespeare to Disney animated films to romantic comedies. They act a shadow version of the hero, and their personality is often a foil to the strengths and weaknesses of the hero.

Writing a Premise Is Hard

If you find this extremely difficult, first, you're not alone. It IS difficult. You might not even know what the heart of your story is yet, and I'm asking you to describe it in a single sentence. So don't be discouraged if you struggle with this or don't get it right.

But if you find that there's NO WAY you can fit your story into a single sentence, that could be a red flag. One common mistake new writers make (and experienced writers, too!) is that we try to fit too much story into one book.

You can't do everything in one novel. The best stories are as narrow and as focused as possible. They don't try to tell everything. They try to tell one story really well.

So if you're struggling with getting your story into a single sentence, ask yourself, *Am I trying to do too much with this story? And if so, can this be split into multiple books? Or do I need to cut out elements so I can focus on what really matters?*

Now, if you've written your premise, and you're ready for the next step in your novel writing process, in the next chapter we're going to explore how to turn your premise into the arc of a story.

Key Ideas

- A premise is a one-sentence summary of your book's main idea. It acts as the foundation for your writing and structuring process.
- A premise in a story contains three things: a protagonist, a goal, and a situation.

Practice

Premise Exercise: Write your story idea as a single-sentence premise containing each of the three elements: a protagonist, a goal, and a situation. For help, you can get the book plan worksheet from The Write Plan planner at thewritepractice.com/structure.

15

FIND YOUR PLOT TYPE

As we go through these steps, I want to reiterate two things:

First, we do not do this work outside of a deadline that's backed up by consequences. Writers can dally around through this process for months and even years. But the purpose of this is not to create more work for yourself, like the equivalent of a celebrity magazine quiz for writing. No, these are tools that help you get to the heart of your story faster, not so that you can admire it and bask in your own brilliance, but so that you can sit down and finish your novel and be confident that your work will bear good fruit.

Second, the purpose of this is not our own fulfillment. We do not do this work for ourselves or to feel good about the writing process, but rather to create something that our readers, our audience, will one day deeply connect with.

As Robert McKee says, "When talented people write badly, it's generally for one of two reasons: either they're blinded by an idea they feel compelled to prove, or they're driven by an emotion they must express. When talented people write well, it is generally for this reason: they're moved by a desire to touch the audience."

In these chapters, you might find your understanding of your book idea challenged, or you might feel like your perfect idea is slipping from you, with perhaps nothing to take its place. Or perhaps it won't be the entire idea, but pieces of the idea that you thought were key to the whole.

If that happens to you, I want you to let it go so as to create room for new ideas, new stories.

Because the purpose of this work that we do is not to feel good about our idea or even to express ourselves (although that's certainly part of the process). The purpose is to connect deeply with our audience, just as our favorite writers have created books that have connected with us.

The righteous, as the psalm says, give without sparing.

What Is Your Story's Type?

Once you've written your story's premise, the next step is to discover your story's core and sub-types.

As we talked about in Chapter 4, your story's type is linked to the values at work in your story.

Here, again, are the types and their related value scales.

Plot Types

1. **Life vs. Death:** Action, Adventure
2. **Life vs. a Fate *Worse* than Death:** Thriller, Horror, Mystery/Crime
3. **Love vs. Hate:** Love Story, Romance
4. **Accomplishment vs. Failure:** Performance, Sports
5. **Maturity vs. Naïveté:** Coming-of-Age
6. **Good vs. Evil:** Temptation, Morality

How do you find *your* story's type, though?

It's one thing to look at a list of twelve plot types, and it's another thing to know how they work in *your* story.

In this chapter, I will share the three-step process you can use to find your story's type. Then, we will go deeper into each of these types and the values at work in them, so that you can more easily identify the type at work in your story. Finally, once you know your type, we'll talk about how to use it to begin the process of outlining your story.

But first, I want to address an objection you might be feeling about plot types in general.

Are Plot Types Just Putting Your Story in a Box?

"Isn't this just putting stories in a box?" some writers ask me. "Where does this leave room for creativity?"

If you're having an aversion to plot types, just know you're not alone. I get the feeling, and honestly, I used to have similar aversions.

I will also say that some story structure frameworks *do* put writers in a box, but what's so great about The Write Structure is that it's flexible enough to help you describe any story you want to tell while also giving you an objective framework to understand whether your story is accomplishing your goals.

You can use this process to write an eight-book series with every plot type possible, or you can use it to write a short story with just one type.

And while there are some recommendations for each type and how to combine them based on what has worked well for other books, it's completely up to you how you use them.

In other words, this process is descriptive, not prescriptive, but once you can describe the story *you're* trying to tell through this framework, it gives you a much better sense of what in your story is working and what isn't.

If You're Stuck on Plot Type: 3 Steps to Figure it Out

Figuring out your story's type can be one of the most important and challenging parts of the Write Structure process. It's here where you can have some of the biggest breakthroughs for your writing, and it's also the place where you can become the most confused.

Here, I want to give you a simple three-step process that will help you get to the heart of your story without fail, especially if you're struggling.

1. Start with Value

Some stories are easy. They neatly line up into their core values.

Others, not so much.

The Write Structure process assumes that all values found in any story can be found in the six *core* values: survival, safety, love and belonging, esteem, self-actualization, and transcendence.

But what if you don't see *your* story in those six? And furthermore, how do you find your way from that value to your plot type?

Just as human values can be expressed in an infinite number of ways, so stories are infinitely variable, and types reflect that variability within some tried-and-true patterns.

Below are some other words you might use for your story's value.

Other Words You Might Use for the Core Values

Before we get into these values, a warning: it's easy to get lost in this complexity. If this happens to you, go back to the basics, the six values, and find your way from there.

I will include the full list below. Keep in mind, this is a work in progress, and some values may not be represented here.

The point of this list is to show that many of the words we use to describe our stories and to describe our plot type still come back to the six values.

- **Status:** Can be a combination of all the lower values, Survival + Safety + Belonging + Esteem. Plot type: sometimes combined with Self-Actualization to create a coming-of-age or hero's journey story. There are very few straight status stories, because it's hard to pull off all of them in one story. Example: *Hamilton* (musical)
- **Justice:** A version of the value of Safety (in reverse). Scale: Life versus a Fate Worse than Death. The true value at the core of every crime and mystery plot type, justice is an extension of safety occurring when a victim has been made *unsafe*, either by being hurt, the victim of theft, or killed. Justice is an act of restoring safety to society, finding the perpetrator, and ensuring no one else becomes their victim. Thus, justice is on the life vs. a fate *worse* than death value scale. Even though the value has a slightly different name, it still finds its way back to that scale. It's also no coincidence that in many crime or mystery stories, the detective finds themselves in near-death situations, becoming the victim or near-victim of the very perpetrator they are working to expose and bring to justice.
- **Freedom:** Survival + Self-Actualization/Society-Actualization
- **Power (as in Might, the personal ability to protect oneself and others):** Safety + Self-Actualization
- **Belonging:** Love + Self-Actualization
- **Influence:** Esteem + Self-Actualization
- **Sacrifice:** Survival/Safety + Transcendence

- **Honor:** Safety + Transcendence
- **Brotherhood (in war):** Love + Safety + Transcendence
- **Dignity:** Esteem + Transcendence
- **Hero's Journey:** Status + Self-Actualization (often with a dose of Transcendence at the end)

2. Look at the Big Event

If you still haven't figured out your core value or plot type, look at your big event.

The big event is the climax of the story and is dependent both on your story's type and also on the inciting incident your story began with.

Here are common big events for each plot type:

- **Action: Battle over the MacGuffin.** A final battle occurs between the protagonist and their team versus the antagonist and their henchmen over an object or person of central importance to the plot.
- **Adventure: Final Battle.** A final battle occurs, whether it's a grand battle between two armies, a smaller battle between the protagonist's party and the antagonist's, or a one-on-one battle to the death.
- **Thriller: At the Mercy of the Villain.** The protagonist, in pursuing the antagonist, finds themself caught by the villain and is at their mercy before escaping due to a mistake by the villain, luck, trickery, or sheer grit.
- **Horror: At the Mercy of the Monster.** This is the same as "At the Mercy of the Villain" except the villain is a monstrous creature.
- **Mystery/Crime: Confession of the Crime.** The protagonist, upon solving the crime, summarizes it

to the villain, who confesses and implicates themselves in the crime.
- **Love: Proof of Love.** The protagonist, having been separated from their true love, performs a final, desperate act to prove their love.
- **Performance: The Big Competition.** The protagonist performs in a final competition, proving their talent and determination, and demonstrating the lessons gained in the course of the story.
- **Coming-of-Age: Breakdown.** The protagonist's old worldview suffers complete breakdown and, in a moment of insight built up by the previous events in the story, is replaced with a new, more advanced worldview.
- **Temptation/Morality: Final Judgment.** The protagonist is judged for their actions, and to the extent they give in to temptation, suffer the consequences, or to the extent they resist temptation and perform good, receive the rewards.

While this is by no means an exhaustive list of all the possible climatic events, it should give you a good sense of how a story's type affects the climax.

Now, think through your story idea. Does your story have any of these big events? Or even several? If it does, you begin to have clues as to your plot type.

3. Decide What You Want Your Readers to Take Away from Your Story

If at this point, you still aren't sure what your story's type is, you must go back to your original intentions for writing the story in the first place.

What is it you're trying to do with your story? What do you

want your readers to feel? What larger point about the world do you want them to take away from the story?

Spend some time thinking through your purpose behind the story, even talking it through with a friend, fellow writer, or editor.

This process may take some time as you filter through your feelings around your story, but hopefully the values, and thus the type, will begin to emerge.

Is this feeling or a takeaway a life lesson, a moral, a religion, or a worldview?

One warning: be careful if your purpose behind telling your story is a life lesson, a moral, a religion, or a worldview.

If you're trying to tell a story that doesn't line up with one of the six core value scales and you instead are trying to prove a moral, a religious tenet, or a worldview through a story, you run the risk of having no story at all.

This is a common mistake I see from new writers, and it's even a mistake that I've found myself making in the past.

It should be a major red flag to you if by this point you haven't found a core value scale for your story but you *do* have a moral point you're trying to make.

There's nothing wrong with offering life lessons, presenting moral or religious points, or sharing a worldview. These line up in the self-actualization value, since self-actualization is all about becoming fully who you are, often by following a specific code, moral framework, or worldview.

But if that's all your story is, then it's not enough. Self-actualization on its own, apart from a combination with a more external value scale, is how-to nonfiction at best or propaganda at worst.

The Most Common Mistakes Writers Make When it Comes to Their Plot Types

As I've walked writers through this process, I've found that they make a few common mistakes with plot types, but the biggest mistake by far is that they don't include an external plot type.

As a reminder:

External plot types are about external values that involve the *body* or *external relationships*.

Internal plot types are about internal values, things happening within you, like your *identity*, *worldview*, and *morality*.

Here are the external and internal plot types and value scales:

External

- **Action/Adventure:** Life vs. Death
- **Horror, Thriller, Crime:** Life (safety) vs. a Fate Worse than Death
- **Love/Romance:** Love vs. Hate
- **Performance, Sports:** Accomplishment vs. Failure

Internal

- **Coming-of-Age:** Self-actualization vs. Immaturity
- **Temptation:** Good vs. Evil

As we talked about in Chapter 4, the external plot types and values *tend* to be the types of most commercial, best-selling stories. There's a reason for that, because those external values are where much of life's conflict originates. It's not that you can't have *internal* conflict, but almost always, internal conflict begins from external sources.

By increasing *external* conflict, you increase *internal* conflict.

Don't misunderstand me.

You *can* have a story where the main plot is internal.

However, if you *only* focus on the internal, you may not have much of a story, because there won't be enough external conflict to drive the internal conflict.

Here's a sign that you're making this mistake in your writing: too many "café scenes"

When I first started working on my memoir about living in Paris, my plan was to write a book about what it was like to sit in the cafés where Joyce and Hemingway and Stein wrote, to soak in the atmosphere, to walk the streets filled with so much literary history, and to write there.

I wanted to focus on the internal, in other words.

It sounded great to me, but my writer friends pushed back on the idea.

"That sounds like a pretty boring book," people told me again and again.

That's a danger many writers face when they focus on the internal, when they talk about the family history of their characters, the life transformation they go through, their personal growth and maturing process.

They end up writing a lot of "café scenes," scenes where the character is sitting around talking with someone else, or worse, sitting around by themselves and thinking about something.

Think about your favorite books and films.

They might have one or two café scenes, but those scenes are the exception. Most of the story involves characters *doing* something. They might be talking, they might be exploring the depths of their identity and life itself, but they aren't just sitting around.

The Solution: External Subplot(s)

If your main plot is internal and you're finding that you have too many café scenes, the plot isn't moving enough, and readers are telling you it's boring, you have three options:

1. **Add an external subplot:** A good example of this is *The Life of Pi*, in which the main plot is an internal coming-of-age plot about a young boy discovering his place in the world and within several religious traditions, but which also has a strong external adventure plot involving a shipwreck and long period of being lost at sea with a murderous tiger who may or may not have been actually a person.
2. **Add several external subplots:** Alternatively, add several external subplots. Some internally-driven stories don't settle on *one* external subplot, but rely on several to keep them moving. *Catcher in the Rye* and *Charlotte's Web* are two well known examples of this, both of which are coming-of-age stories and both of which have several almost episodic adventure plot threads that weave through the story.

Internally-driven stories can be masterpieces. But unless you have a level of external plot, most readers will put it down.

Instead, add threads of external plot, or one external subplot, to bolster your conflict and create a story that readers can't put down.

Alternatively, consider writing nonfiction or allegorical fiction.

If you're still struggling to layer your internal plot with external subplots or threads, consider whether nonfiction how-to/self-help or allegorical fiction (like *The Go-Giver* or *The Ultimate Gift*) would be a better fit for you.

If your goal is less to tell an entertaining story and more to teach, there are other literary forms that work better for that goal.

I have seen so many writers bend over backward trying to make their story work, trying to make it interesting and entertaining, when their original goal behind writing the story was to inspire and teach, *not* to entertain.

Be honest with yourself and your goals, and if another format would be better for you, then do it.

Plot Type is Freeing

Many writers feel constrained by plot types, especially when they're not sure what their plot type is.

But plot type can also be incredibly freeing, a tool to better understand what is happening in your story and make sure it matches what you want the reader to experience.

You can view it as "paint by numbers," or you can view it as the art tradition you're working within, and like any artist, you can choose where to push the boundaries and where you want to embrace that tradition and make it your own.

"The hard truth is that books are made from books," said Cormac McCarthy.

Because what you should *not* do is pretend that the book you're writing exists *apart* from tradition, which is an arrogant, ineffective, and ultimately inefficient approach.

Instead, know the plot types, use the plot types, and if you can, transcend the plot types.

Key Ideas

- Plot types, and the Write Structure process as a whole, are descriptive, not prescriptive. They're a way to better understand the story you're trying to tell, not a way to "put your story in a box."
- To determine your story's plot type, start with the

values at stake, then look at the story's big event, and finally, ask yourself what you want the reader to take away from the story.
- If your takeaway is a life lesson, a moral, a religious point, or a worldview, consider whether writing nonfiction or allegorical fiction might be a better avenue for your project.
- If your main plot is driven by an internal value, be sure to add external subplots to give your story more action and drama.

16

PLOT YOUR STORY IN 18 SENTENCES

Outlining can be a dreaded word for some writers, but whether you're a pantser or a planner a simple outline will help you when the writing gets hard.

Writers so often get lost in their drafts. You're writing along, making quick progress into exciting new territories, and then all of a sudden you finish a chapter or a plot point and you have no idea what comes next.

From there, it's easy to get completely derailed, filling your writing time with procrastination—Facebook, minor household chores, sudoku—because you can't admit to yourself that you're completely lost.

An outline is a life raft. Alone, it can't completely save you, but it can help you get your head above water and start to make your way to safety.

That's why I believe that even if you're a panster, you will find the writing process much easier if you create a simple outline. All it needs to contain is everything you think you know about the story. If that's just a few sentences, all the better.

If you don't have an idea, use our guide to best book ideas

on The Write Practice (thewritepractice.com/best-novel-ideas) to come up with one.

How I Structure My Story

Any time I start a new novel or memoir, or any time I *edit* a book, I use these ideas.

I start by writing out the six elements of plot. I put colons after each one, like this:

Exposition:
Inciting Incident:
Rising Action:
Dilemma:
Climax:
Denouement:

If I'm feeling really ambitious, I create a spreadsheet like this:

6 Sentence Outline

	Exposition
	Inciting Incident
Core Story	Rising Action
	Dilemma
	Climax
	Denouement

I still don't write yet. Instead, I think.

Six sentences. That's all it takes. But these are not easy sentences.

What *is* the inciting incident? What *are* the dilemma and the climax?

When I'm working on a first draft this is actually pretty easy.

Not because I have all the answers, no. But because I have enough answers to feel like I have it pretty much figured out.

It's harder when I'm working on a second or third draft.

Then, I *should* know what's in my book, that I *wrote*, that took me several months to write.

But I often don't know. Maybe I sort of do, but not really.

This is the hard part, the second draft, when you have to sort through the chaos and try to make sense of it.

It's easier if you start with some of this structure already, but even then, there's a lot to sift through.

How I Structure My Book In 18 Sentences

As we've talked about, every story contains the six elements of plot, but just the same, every *act* contains the six elements.

And if we're going to write a one-sentence outline for each, that means we need eighteen sentences, like this:

18 Sentence Outline

	Exposition
	Inciting Incident
Act 1	Rising Action
	Dilemma
	Climax
	Denouement
	Exposition
	Inciting Incident
Act 2	Rising Action
	Dilemma
	Climax
	Denouement
	Exposition
	Inciting Incident
Act 3	Rising Action
	Dilemma
	Climax
	Denouement

2020 © The Write Practice

(By the way, I created The Write Plan planner to make this process easier. Check it out at thewritepractice.com/planner.)

Before I start a first draft, I might not have eighteen sentences. I might only know enough of what's going to happen for ten or eleven scenes.

The point, in a first draft, isn't to fill in the entire outline. It's just to write what you know.

In a second or third draft, though, I should have a clear picture of the eighteen sentences. Which is to say, I spend a lot of time looking at this spreadsheet before beginning!

When I move on to the next phase depends on my confidence level. When I'm writing a first draft, I'm fairly confident, mostly because I don't really know anything!

In a second draft, this process takes me a long time. Months, even.

For me, a first draft is like mining a block of marble. The second draft is like chiseling out a sculpture. Whereas the first draft is all hard labor, the second is thinking work.

But as you fill in your eighteen-sentence outline, you might be wondering where your subplot should fit. Let's look at how subplots tend to fit within the three-act structure.

Where Subplots Fit Within Your Outline

A traditional three-act story has one core plot, and the core plot will have each of the six elements scattered throughout the story. For example, if you look at a typical story, the core plot's elements might fit through the book as follows (core plot elements in bold):

Act 1: Introduce the world and characters, and begin the main plot

- **Core Exposition**
- **Core Inciting Incident**
- Rising Action

- Dilemma
- Climax
- Denouement

Act 2: Complicate the plot through the rising action

- Exposition
- Inciting Incident
- **Core Rising Action**
- **Core Dilemma**
- Climax
- Denouement

Act 3: Pay off the plot with the climax and resolution

- Exposition
- Inciting Incident
- Rising Action
- Core dilemma
- **Core Climax**
- **Core Denouement**

However, as you can see, there are more instances of exposition and rising action than there are core plots. Many of these additional sections of exposition and rising action can be filled by the subplot.

See below (subplot elements underlined):

Act 1: Introduce the world, characters, and begin the main plot

- **Core Exposition**
- **Core Inciting Incident**
- Rising Action
- Dilemma
- Climax

- Denouement

Act 2: Complicate the plot through the rising action

- Subplot Exposition
- Subplot Inciting Incident
- **Core Rising Action** Subplot Rising Action
- **Core Dilemma**
- Climax / Subplot dilemma *(sometimes)*
- Denouement

Act 3: Pay off the plot with the climax and resolution

- Exposition
- Inciting Incident
- Rising Action
- Dilemma
- **Core Climax**
- **Core Denouement** / Subplot Climax and Denouement

In the three-act structure, subplots usually, but not always, begin right at the second act, like we see marked above and underlined. They often progress quickly in the inciting incident and rising action.

Then, in the climactic moment of act two, just when you think everything should go well, a giant question mark is thrown into them.

In a love story subplot, this is often when we wonder *whether* the couple will actually get together in the end. Can they get past the things that are keeping them apart and finally connect?

In an adventure subplot, this might be a major setback, when you wonder whether the goal the characters are working toward will ever be achieved.

Whatever happens, the subplot, which seemed to be going so strong, all of a sudden stops dead, and the audience is left to forget about it for a while.

The subplot might come back briefly here and there through to the third act, but it's usually not resolved until the final scene, one of the *most* effective moments to bring things together, when the subplot has its climactic moment and final denouement and resolution.

The above is just an example, and subplots find their ways in many other shapes and sizes. However, this can be a good general template for using a subplot in your story.

Use Subplots to Fill In Your Story

A great subplot will not save your lagging story. For a story to work, both the core plot *and* subplot must be working together to draw the reader through the rises and falls in the values of the story arc.

However, even the best stories can feel somewhat empty in the middle act alone. After all, it's easy for an author to run out of ideas, and for the characters to run out of drama to create.

Instead, fill that space with a subplot, and let it carry the burden of the middle of your story.

How I Structure Each Scene

Any time I start a new scene in a novel or a memoir, and any time I *edit* a scene or chapter, I use the ideas in this book.

I start by creating a new document in Scrivener[1], which is the word processor I use to write my books, or opening up a scene that I've already written.

Then, before I start writing or editing, I open up the right-sidebar inspector to the notes tab and write the following:

The Write Structure

Story Event:
Setting:
Exposition:
Inciting Incident:
Rising Action:
Dilemma:
Climax:
Denouement:

I write those words exactly (careful to remember that extra "e" in denouement).

Because a story isn't just made up of six or even eighteen sentences. The same six elements of plot that you need in the story and in each act are needed in each scene as well.

Here's how it looks in Scrivener:

I still don't write. A few more minutes of thinking and planning is all it takes to write a great scene.

I think, *What is actually happening in this scene?*

Where is this scene set? How does it start?

And what begins the action?

How do the events get more and more complicated?

What is the dilemma? And how does the dilemma build into the climax?

Finally, what is the denouement?

If I don't know *any* of these, I start with the story event and dilemma. Often, if you know the dilemma, the rest of the scene can become clear (this is especially true when you're working on difficult rewrites and second drafts).

I also make sure not to forget the denouement, as it can be really easy to end a scene at the climax and not wrap things up.

Then Write

Write.

Write imperfectly.

Write like no one will ever read it.

Write like you know you'll be able to come back and fix all your mistakes, because you will.

Write as quickly as you can.

Even if you're rewriting, write quickly because it's best to not think too much.

You've done your thinking.

Now is the time for writing, for discovery, for finding out what is *actually* going to happen in this story. Everything else, all that planning you did, all of that doesn't matter because this mysterious magical thing that is happening under your fingers is where the magic happens.

Write like you breathe; inhale everything around you and exhale words and life and magic. It doesn't have to be perfect. I'll say it again: It doesn't have to be perfect. Perfect is for planning and for editors.

Writing is life and life is never perfect.

Write anyway.

Write.

Just write.

I say it three times because sometimes you have to

remember to just write and not worry about the plan and living up to it.

Your outline sentences can be a great burden, because how can you ever live up to them?

Don't try. Just write.

Besides, if you do this right, your subconscious will take care of the plan anyway, and maybe a whole new, better plan will form.

Write and you will learn. Write and you will practice.

This. Right here. Is the best part.

Enjoy it.

But You Sometimes Won't

Sometimes, the words don't come.

You get lost in them.

What *actually* needs to happen here?

What is this scene *really* about?

And here your sentences can be a great comfort, your outline a lighthouse in the midst of the storm.

Come back to them. Just write the next sentence in the outline. Don't worry about the whole. Just worry about that one small sentence. It's just a sentence, after all.

You don't have to fix everything right now.

This is a long slog, a daily dragging yourself to the keyboard. This is where the grit comes in.

But without it, there will be no finished book.

Key Ideas

- Outlining your book can be done in as little as eighteen sentences but it will help both planners and pantsers finish a great book.
- Outline with one sentence for each of the six elements of plot: exposition, inciting incident, rising

action, dilemma, climax, and denouement.
- Since each story, act, and scene contains each of the six elements, and most stories should follow the three-act structure, you can create an eighteen sentence outline with six sentences for each act.
- For first drafts, focus primarily on finding the dilemma, especially if outlining feels like it's impeding your flow.

Practice

Outlining Exercise One: Start by writing out a six-sentence outline, one sentence for each element: exposition, inciting incident, rising action, dilemma, climax, and denouement. To aid this process, you can find an excerpt worksheet from The Write Plan planner in our bonus content at thewritepractice.com/structure.

Outlining Exercise Two: Then, outline each act with six sentences for each of the three acts.

Outlining Exercise Three: Finally, if you choose to create a scene outline, you can write a six sentence outline for each scene. Again, find a worksheet to do this at thewritepractice.com/structure.

17
HOW TO WRITE A GOOD FIRST CHAPTER

For the writer, there's nothing harder than writing the first chapter and the final chapter of a book. It is here that all of your perfectionism rears its ugly head, calling for a full halt to your progress.

I've written and rewritten my first chapter dozens of times, and I'm not alone. Most writers struggle to figure out how to start their novel, and it makes sense. Your first chapter can make or break your book with readers, agents, *and* publishers.

So then, how do you do it? How do you write a good first chapter?

In this chapter, I'm going to walk you through the ten things you need to accomplish in your first chapter, and I'll give you a checklist that you can use in your novel.

Why Does It Matter if the First Chapter Is Good?

My dad recently finished a new book and wants to submit it to agents. So, dutiful son that I am, I helped him find a short list of agents on querytracker.com and talked him through their submission requirements.

Each of these literary agents' submission requirements

varied, but nearly all of them asked for the first few pages, anywhere between the first three chapters to the first ten pages.

Agents, who often get thousands of submissions per month, will tell you how much those first pages matter.

If those first pages don't hook them, if they don't instantly capture their attention and make them want to read more, they'll move on to the next submission.

That means, if you want your book to be picked up by an agent and then a publisher, your first chapter needs to be good.

That means this chapter has a lot of heavy lifting to do, story-wise.

So, I thought, *what exactly do writers need to accomplish in their first chapter? What is your First Chapter Checklist?*

One thing to keep in mind, though: books that have a prologue may not achieve *all* of these things in the first chapter.

Checklist: 6 Steps to Write a Good First Chapter

How do you write a good first chapter? If you touch each of these things, you're sure to hook the reader and create a strong foundation for your book.

1. Set the Scene through Physical Movement

Before you can get into the action and drama of a scene, the reader needs to know when and where they are. Publishers, agents, and readers alike don't enjoy being thrown into the middle of a disorienting action scene. Instead, they prefer to let the scene build up to a climactic moment using the six elements of storytelling (see #6), beginning with a brief amount of exposition.

The best way to set the scene is not through description, which readers, agents, and publishers alike find off-putting in the first sentences of the first scene; or through dialogue, which leaves readers confused. *Wait, who's talking?*

Instead, begin with a character making some kind of physical action through the space that reveals the broader context of the scene.

2. Introduce the Protagonist

Your protagonist is the lens through which you tell your story, so introduce them to the reader in the very first scene.

But it's not enough for the reader to simply *see* the protagonist. We have to *like them* enough to want to follow them for the rest of the story.

That doesn't mean you can't have a protagonist who is flawed or even evil. It *does* mean we have to sympathize with them.

Here are seven tried-and-true ways to get your reader to sympathize with your characters. I recommend picking at least one to use in your first chapter and three in your first few chapters.

The 7 Characteristics of Sympathetic Characters

1. **Takes action.** Show your protagonist being proactive. Show them making a hard choice when faced with a dilemma and taking action to get what they want.
2. **Treated unjustly.** Show your character being bullied, persecuted, treated unfairly, or made the victim of injustice.
3. **Shows competence.** Readers are interested in people who are really good at things. Don't hide your protagonist's light under a bushel. Let it shine!
4. **Has friends.** We're attracted to people who show that they already have other people who like them. Just them having a friend makes us more interested in them. Show your protagonist is likeable by

surrounding them with other interesting characters from the beginning.
5. **Does a good deed.** "Save the cat," as Blake Snyder says. By showing your protagonist helping someone in need, you establish them as "the good guy," despite any other negative qualities.
6. **Has a humanizing quirk.** Quirks are memorable things that both let us create an instant visualization of someone *and* humanize the character, like Harry Potter's scar on his forehead, Ron Weasley's bright red hair, or Hermione's frizzy hair. Quirks can be mannerisms, too, like Elizabeth Bennet's penchant for long walks or Anne from *Anne of Green Gables*'s habit of speaking in very long sentences. Quirks are especially important for side characters, but a simple quirk helps us quickly get to know a protagonist. They also can humanize an otherwise flat character.
7. **Has a secret vulnerability.** Everyone has a secret, whether it's a phobia like Bruce Wayne's fear of bats or Superman's weakness toward kryptonite or Inspector Gamache's terror of heights. By letting the reader in on your protagonist's secret vulnerability, you create a bond that can last the entire story.

You can use these seven characteristics of sympathetic characters at any point in your story for any character, even your villains. They are like candy for readers, and they will always get results.

However, these characteristics are *most* important to use in the first chapter when you need to *quickly* create a connection with your protagonist. In fact, you could argue that this is the *whole goal* of the first chapter.

3. Set the Genre

Establish the type of story you're writing from the beginning. From the first scene, your reader should know whether this is a science fiction story, a crime novel, a horror novel, or a love story.

4. Set the Value Scale

In the same way, establish the value scale that your novel will move on. As we've discussed, there are traditionally six value scales, each of which relates to particular types of stories:

1. **Life vs. Death:** Action, Adventure
2. **Life vs. a Fate *Worse* than Death:** Thriller, Horror, Mystery
3. **Love vs. Hate:** Love Story, Romance
4. **Accomplishment vs. Failure:** Performance, Sports
5. **Maturity vs. Naïveté:** Coming-of-Age
6. **Good vs. Evil:** Temptation, Morality

Once you know which plot type you're telling, make sure your first scene is set on that scale.

For example, in a love story, make sure the story event occurring in the very first scene deals either with love or hate. Or in a coming-of-age story, set it in a moment of great immaturity.

5. Set the Stakes

Once your value scale is set, create some kind of movement, ideally moving to either the very bottom or very top of that scale.

For example, in an action story, have a moment where your protagonist is almost sure to die.

Or in a love story, begin in a place of complete hatred between the principal characters.

By setting the stakes early, you let the reader know what to expect (and how you're going to play with those expectations).

6. Follow the 6 Elements of Plot

As we've discussed, every successful scene, act, and story has six elements of plot that make it work:

1. Exposition
2. Inciting Incident
3. Rising Action/Progressive Complications
4. Dilemma
5. Climax
6. Denouement

Remember that the most important of these six is the dilemma, when a character is faced with a difficult choice between two equally good or equally bad options.

This dilemma is what causes the movement of the scene along your value scale and what creates the essential drama.

All that to say, make sure your first chapter has each of these, but especially the dilemma!

The Essentials of a Good First Chapter

Don't be a perfectionist with your first chapter, especially if you're writing a first draft.

First drafts are hard. First drafts of first chapters are *really* hard.

Don't try to write a publishable, award-winning, New York Times best-selling first chapter the first time you sit down to work on your new story.

Instead, just do the work.

Set the scene with action.

Introduce your protagonist in a sympathetic way so your readers can fall in love with them.

Set the genre and value scale.

Hit each of the six elements.

If you do that, you'll have a strong first chapter that you can make even better in revision.

Key Ideas

- Both literary agents and readers evaluate books based on the quality of the first chapter.
- In the first chapter you must set the scene, introduce a sympathetic protagonist, identify the genre, set the value scale, set the story stakes, and follow the six elements of plot.

Practice

First Chapter Exercise: Use the first chapter checklist with *your* story. Go back and review a first chapter that you've written. Or if you haven't written a first chapter yet, outline a new one! Does it hit all six steps of the checklist? Which of the seven characteristics of sympathetic characters does it touch on? What is it missing? What can you change in it to make sure you hit all of the steps?

CONCLUSION: BUILDING A DEFINITION OF STORIES

This book came out of a process of trying to figure out my own books.

A book is just a big problem, remember?

Story structure, these plot diagrams we've been talking about, are just a way to take a big problem, that is, a book, and break it up into a lot of smaller problems.

Just write the next sentence. Just solve the next little problem.

If a story is six sentences, each act is six sentences, each scene is six sentences, and a story is usually fifty to seventy scenes, that means all you need to do is solve three to four hundred problems.

If you do that, you'll have a story.

Not so hard, right?

Who can't write three to four hundred sentences?

So may you structure your story soundly, may you plot your diagrams clearly, but most of all, may you write.

Good luck, and happy writing.

MORE RESOURCES

1) The Write Structure Bonus Resources
To get the most out of The Write Structure process, download a set of worksheets and tutorials at
thewritepractice.com/structure

2) The Write Plan Planner
The Write Structure and The Write Plan planner go hand in hand. Once you've learned the principles of structure, put it to practice with your book using this beautifully designed planner that combines everything we've learned about how to *finish* a book over the last decade. Get the planner at
thewritepractice.com/planner.

3) 100 Day Book
We built 100 Day Book to give writers the mentorship, accountability, and encouragement to finish a great book in 100 Days . We'd love to join your team and encourage and support you in 100 Day Book. Check it out and sign up at
thewritepractice.com/100-day-book.

APPENDIX A: WHY FREYTAG'S TECHNIQUE DOESN'T WORK

Most great stories, whether they are a Pixar film or a novel by your favorite author, follow a certain dramatic structure.

When you're getting started with writing, understanding how structure works is difficult. Even if you go back and analyze your favorite books and films, it can still be hard to decipher how the author is making the story work.

Then, once you find the dramatic structure of your favorite stories, how do you structure your stories in a similar way without ripping off another writer?

One of the oldest and most helpful dramatic structures for story was developed by Gustav Freytag in the mid-19th century. This structure has become known as Freytag's Pyramid, and it has become so ubiquitous, many of the best writers have used it to write their own stories, even if they didn't know it was called Freytag's Pyramid.

In this Appendix, we're going to look at Freytag's Pyramid and talk about what it is; whether it would be helpful to use as you structure the plot of your own stories, books, and screenplays; what its limitations are as a dramatic structure; and what other popular plot structure alternatives exist.

Appendix A: Why Freytag's Technique Doesn't Work

What is Freytag's Pyramid?

Freytag's Pyramid is a dramatic structural framework developed by Gustav Freytag, a German author of the mid-19th century. He theorized that effective stories could be broken into two halves, the play and counterplay, with the climax in the middle.

These two halves create a pyramid or triangle shape containing five dramatic elements: introduction, rising movement, climax, falling movement, and denouement or catastrophe.

Freytag's Pyramid Plot Diagram

The pyramid, sometimes called Freytag's Triangle, is best visualized in the following diagram:

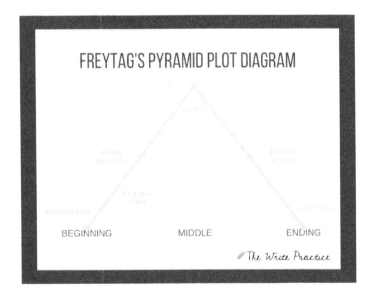

How to Understand Freytag's Pyramid

Gustav Freytag originally formulated Freytag's Pyramid in his 1863 book *Freytag's Technique of the Drama*, and over the last more than 150 years, it has become one of the most commonly taught dramatic structures in the world, finding its way into thousands of classrooms and writing workshops.

Here's the original plot diagram (found on page 115 of *Freytag's Technique*):

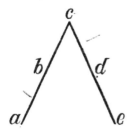

These parts of the drama, (*a*) introduction, (*b*) rise, (*c*) climax, (*d*) return or fall, (*e*) catastrophe, have each what is peculiar in purpose and in construction.

I think many of us have a kind of vague sense of this story structure, even if we were never formally taught it.

However, one thing I realized after actually *reading Freytag's Technique* is that the structure that I learned doesn't actually conform to how Freytag thought of it. It surprised me that many of the terms Freytag used are different than those used in subsequent ways of teaching his Pyramid.

For example, many articles on Freytag's Pyramid use the term "denouement" to describe part of the story structure. The word denouement, however, never appears in Freytag's work (not even in the original German).

On top of that, I found that many of the concepts differ radically from how we generally understand them today.

Below, I've tried to summarize Freytag's Pyramid based on how I understood it in *Freytag's Technique*, while also including modern interpretations. But if you're interested in this subject, it would be worth reading his book on your own.

The 5 Elements of Freytag's Pyramid

Here are definitions for the five elements of Freytag's Pyramid:

1. Introduction

The introduction contains both the exposition and "exciting force":

Exposition: This is a set of scenes in which no major changes occur. The point is to introduce the principal characters, time period, and tone, and set up the "exciting force."

Exciting Force: Freytag also calls this the "complication," and other frameworks call it the "inciting incident." It's when some force of will on the part of the protagonist or an outside complication forces the protagonist into motion.

2. Rising Movement

Now that the chief action has been started, this continues the movement toward the climax. Any characters who have not as of yet been introduced should be introduced here.

(Note that many people call this the "rising action," but Freytag calls it rising movement.)

3. Climax

In Freytag's framework, the climax occurs in the middle of the story.

In this framework, the climax can be thought of as a reflection point. If things have gone well for the protagonist, at the climax they start to fall apart tragically.

Or in a comedy, if things have been going poorly for the protagonist, things start improving.

The author should, according to Freytag, put his or her best effort into the writing of this scene, as it is the moment that carries the story as a whole.

The way that Freytag himself talks about this in *Freytag's Technique of the Drama* is much less simplistic. The climax is still the point at which the story reflects and afterward becomes the mirror story, the counter-play.

But rather than just focus on the *fate* of the protagonist, Freytag thinks about the climax as the scene or group of scenes in which the fullest energy of the protagonist is portrayed, whether for good or ill, pathos or pride. After the climax, whatever ambition the protagonist showed is reversed against himself, and whatever suffering she endured is redeemed. In other words, the energy, values, and themes shown in the first half are reversed and undone in the second half.

As Freytag puts it, "This middle, the climax of the play, is the most important place of the structure; the action rises to this; the action falls away from this."

4. Falling Action

Things continue to either devolve for the protagonist or, in the case of a comedy, improve, leading up to the "force of the final suspense," a moment before the catastrophe, when the author projects the final catastrophe and prepares the audience for it.

As Freytag says, "It is well understood that the catastrophe must not come entirely as a surprise to the audience."

But just after this foreshadowing, there must be a moment of suspense where the slim possibility of reversal is hinted at.

"Although rational consideration makes the inherent necessity of his destruction very evident . . . it is an old, unpretentious poetic device, to give the audience for a few moments a prospect of relief. This is done by means of a new slight, suspense."

5. Catastrophe or Denouement

Freytag was chiefly focused on tragedy, not comedy, and he saw the ending phase of a story as the moment of catastrophe, in which the character is finally undone by their own choices, actions, and energy.

While Freytag never uses the word "denouement" in his own framework, people interpreting him have used the term to describe endings with a happy result for the protagonist.

Example of Freytag's Pyramid: Romeo and Juliet

Let's break down how Freytag's Pyramid actually works using an example that most people are familiar with and Freytag himself used, Shakespeare's *Romeo and Juliet*:

Introduction

We start by getting a sense of the rivalry between the Montagues and the Capulets. As Freytag says, "an open street, brawls, and the clatter of swords of hostile parties."

Then we meet the important characters, including Romeo who is getting over an infatuation with another girl; Mercutio, Romeo's bestie; and Tybalt, the Capulet attack dog and cousin to Juliet.

We also meet Juliet, her parents, and her nurse.

Exciting force: Romeo and his posse decide to attend the Capulets' ball.

Some notes:

- The introduction is pretty short, especially compared to the rising movement.

Appendix A: Why Freytag's Technique Doesn't Work

- No major changes occur here until the exciting force.
- The exciting force should be a major change, but Freytag found it to not be strong enough in *Romeo and Juliet*. He says, "If the exciting force is ever too small and weak for him, as in *Romeo and Juliet*, he understands how to strengthen it. Therefore, Romeo, after his conclusion to intrude upon the Capulets, must pronounce his gloomy forebodings before the house."

Rising Movement: The Couple Meets, Gets Married, Then Gets Into Trouble

Freytag identifies four stages in the rising action:

Stage One: The masked ball. Includes Juliet preparing for the ball, Romeo with his posse before sneaking into the ball, Tybalt's anger at the Montagues being present at the ball, Romeo first seeing Juliet, Romeo and Juliet's first conversation, and finally Juliet's debrief with her nurse.

Stage Two: The garden scene. Includes Romeo's friends looking for him and Romeo and Juliet's conversation and decision to get married.

Stage Three: The marriage. Includes four scenes leading up to Friar Laurence marrying the couple and their brief, happy honeymoon.

Stage Four: Tybalt's death. Includes Romeo running into Tybalt. They fight and Tybalt is killed.

A few notes:

- The rising action covers a lot of ground, from the meet cute to the marriage to the major complication in Tybalt's death.
- For some reason, Freytag totally skips over Mercutio's death, which I found surprising.

Mercutio is the man!
- Personally, if I were putting this play into a three-act structure, I would end act one with the garden scene and begin act two with their preparations for marriage. But that's me. The point, though, is that this approach differs from the way most people look at a three-act story structure today. In fact, Freytag was more interested in a five-act structure.

Climax

Juliet urges Rome to flee and Romeo says goodbye to Juliet. A few notes:

- The climax is relatively short, with just one major scene.
- The climax occurs toward the middle of the play (slightly right, maybe ⅗ of the way through the story).
- Honestly, it's not that climactic. Today, most writers would probably call the final death scene the climax, not this scene. Instead, we would call this the midpoint, a turning point leading up to "the dark night of the soul."
- This is when the counter-play begins. In the first half, the play, the lovers unite. In the counter-play, the lovers separate, until ultimately, they are separated by death.

Falling Action

Romeo is in exile. Juliet's parents force her into an engagement with Paris, and to help her avoid it, Friar Laurence helps her fake her own death. Believing his wife is dead, Romeo leaves exile after purchasing poison to end his life from an apothecary.

Force of the final suspense: Romeo faces Paris in the graveyard, kills him, and enters Juliet's tomb. Friar Laurence enters the graveyard behind him.

A few notes:

- Even though this period takes up a significant amount of time, Freytag isn't that concerned about it. In fact, while every other step in the pyramid has its own section, Freytag doesn't even bother creating a section for this, as if he assumes that the scenes in the Falling Action will write themselves.
- Freytag *does* focus on the force of the final suspense, though, and sees it first as a foreshadowing of the final catastrophe and then a momentary possibility of reversal.

Catastrophe

Romeo discovers Juliet, apparently dead, and gives a final speech before he kills himself with poison. Juliet wakes up from her pretend death to discover Romeo dying. They share a final kiss. Juliet ends her life with Romeo's dagger.

Friar Laurence arrives too late to save them. Then the Prince, the Montagues, and the Capulets join them and the Prince condemns their rivalry and calls for a final peace.

Some notes:

- The catastrophe section, like the climax, is quite short, with just the actual catastrophic scene and one scene of fallout from the event.
- Today, most writers would call this scene the climax of the story.

Freytag's Pyramid vs. Modern Dramatic Structures

While Freytag's Pyramid can be helpful for writers, especially those writing tragedy, his framework differs in some significant ways from other dramatic structures, like *Story Grid* or *Save the Cat*.

For example, one of the core differences is the term "climax." Freytag's framework puts the climax in the middle of the story, where it works as the story's major turning point.

For a traditional understanding of three-act story structure —as found in *Story Grid* or *Save the Cat*—what Freytag calls the climax is instead called the "midpoint."

See the diagram below for an example:

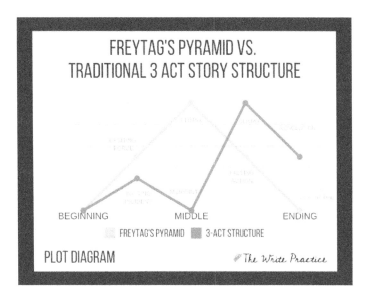

The climax in these frameworks occurs at the end of either the second or third acts, and often is one of the last scenes of the story, taking the location of Freytag's catastrophe.

Freytag also emphasizes the fate and "energy" of the protagonist, whereas The Write Structure emphasizes a character's choice.

Should You Use Freytag's Pyramid?

Maybe.

I think Freytag's Pyramid is most helpful if you're writing tragedy and if you want a framework to help you think through your story from the perspective of two separate halves with a central scene in the middle that acts as a reflection point.

In other words, if you're writing the Icarus story Arc or Man in a Hole story arc.

For other story arcs, The Write Structure is far more flexible, and I no longer recommend Freytag's Pyramid to my writing students as the primary tool for structuring a story.

Beyond just the pyramid, though, I found the majority of *Freytag's Technique of the Drama* to be a fascinating methodology and study of storytelling. The way he understood plot and story structure was unique and challenging, and I got a lot out of reading it.

All that's to say, if you can handle reading a text that was written in the mid-1800s, I would recommend it.[1]

Bonus: Writing Quotes from *Freytag's Technique*

Here are some of my favorite quotes from *Freytag's Technique of the Drama*:

"The poet of the present is inclined to look with amazement upon a method of work in which the structure of scenes, the treatment of characters, and the sequence of effects were governed by a transmitted code of fixed technical rules."

"When the poet has once thus infused his own soul into the material, then he adopts from the real account some things which suit his purpose."

"For thousands of years the human race has thus transposed for itself life in heaven and on earth; it has abundantly endowed its representations of the divine with human attributes. All heroic tradition has sprung from such a transformation of impressions from religious life, history, or natural objects, into poetic ideas."

"The dramatic includes those emotions of the soul which steel themselves to will . . . also the inner processes which man experiences from the first glow of perception to passionate desire and action, as well as the influences which one's own and other's deeds exert upon the soul; also the rushing forth of will power from the depths of man's soul toward the external world, and the influx of fashioning influences from the outer world into man's inmost being; also the coming into being of a deed, and its consequences on the human soul."

"An action, in itself, is not dramatic. Passionate feeling, in itself, is not dramatic. Not the presentation of a passion for itself, but of a passion which leads to action is the business of dramatic art; not the presentation of an event for itself, but for its effect on a human soul is the dramatist's mission. The exposition of passionate emotions as such, is in the province of the lyric poet; the depicting of thrilling events is the task of the epic poet."

"Through this linking together of incidents, dramatic idealization is effected."

"What history is able to declare can be to the poet only the frame within which he paints his most brilliant colors, the most secret revelations of human nature."

"The action of the serious drama must possess importance and magnitude."

"The structure of the drama must show these two contrasted elements of the dramatic joined in a unity, efflux and influx of will-power, the accomplishment of a deed and its reaction on the soul, movement and counter-movement, strife and counter-strife, rising and sinking, binding and loosing."

APPENDIX B: WHY YOU SHOULDN'T USE FALLING ACTION IN YOUR STORY

A Brief History of Falling Action

The term "falling action" was popularized by Gustav Freytag, whom you will now know by name if you didn't before reading this book.

However, you might be able to guess what I'm about to say next: the way Freytag understood story structure is radically different from how it's taught today.

Freytag believed every story contains two halves, a play and a counterplay, with the climax in the middle.

FREYTAG'S PYRAMID PLOT DIAGRAM

To use *Romeo and Juliet* as an example, the climax, according to Freytag, occurs right after Romeo kills Tybalt in retaliation for Tybalt killing Mercutio. Romeo's punishment is exile, and Freytag says the climax is when Romeo and Juliet part ways.

However, most people analyzing that story today, even the ones who feel like they understand Freytag's Pyramid, would say that the climax occurs when Romeo commits suicide, mistakenly thinking Juliet is dead, and Juliet, waking up to him dying, commits suicide in response.

In other words, the climax as we understand it today occurs *much* later in the story.

Freytag's Climax: Romeo and Juliet parting
Modern Climax: Romeo and Juliet's suicide

Falling Action Implications

What this means for the falling action is that in Freytag's original pyramid the falling action actually contained quite a few scenes, about ⅖ of the story.

However, in the modern understanding of story structure, the falling action contains exactly *one* scene.

One.

And that's *if* you combine the falling action with the resolution. If you say the falling action isn't the resolution, that means that the falling action doesn't exist at all.

Which is to say that if you use this model, as most of us do, the falling action is a really unhelpful term.

Freytag *himself* didn't much care for this piece of the dramatic structure, and doesn't even include a section on it in his book *Freytag's Technique of the Drama*.

How the Falling Action Actually Works in Modern Storytelling Structure

The image below is the way most people think of storytelling today, and by the way, this structure is used even by people who claim to be using Freytag's pyramid to diagram their plots:

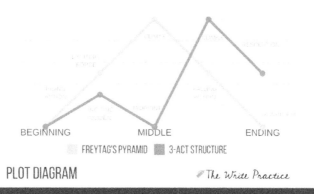

Notice that while there is still a "falling action," in most of the stories used as examples for this structure, there are really only two or three scenes following the climax.

If one of those scenes is the resolution, that means the falling action is just one or two scenes long.

One or two scenes do not need their own story structure element. Especially considering the rising action can contain forty or *more* scenes.

Can we just be honest with ourselves and say that while a resolution is a real thing, and an important part of the structure of stories, falling action doesn't actually exist in modern story structure?

Alternatively, we could just stop pretending that we're using Freytag's Pyramid when we mean something completely different.

NOTES

6. Story Arcs: The 6 Shapes of Stories

1. Find the full study, "Toward a Science of Human Stories," here (the section on story arcs begins on page 73): https://arxiv.org/abs/1712.06163
2. Check out his 2014 article, "Cracking the Sitcom Code," in *The Atlantic*: https://www.theatlantic.com/entertainment/archive/2014/12/cracking-the-sitcom-code/384068/

8. Element 2: Inciting Incident

1. The original Wired article is here https://www.wired.com/2011/09/mf-harmon, but you can also find a longer discussion of Harmon's story theory on this Medium article by Scott Distillery https://scottdistillery.medium.com/dan-harmon-the-heros-journey-and-the-circle-theory-of-story-b64bb77d6976.

10. Element 4: Dilemma

1. Thorough summary of studies done on the effect of storytelling on the brain: https://www.nytimes.com/2012/03/18/opinion/sunday/the-neuroscience-of-your-brain-on-fiction.html

16. Plot Your Story In 18 Sentences

1. Find my review of Scrivener (and why I prefer to use it to write books over Word) here: https://thewritepractice.com/scrivener

Appendix A: Why Freytag's Technique Doesn't Work

1. You can read *Freytag's Technique of the Drama* for free here: https://books.google.com/books?id=nD8PAQAAMAAJ.

Made in the USA
Las Vegas, NV
09 September 2022